ADVENTURING

ADVENTURING

IT IS NOT JUST FOR THE YOUNG AND STRONG

Charting Pathways
To
A Richer Life

John R. Hook

iUniverse, Inc.
Bloomington

ADVENTURING
IT IS NOT JUST FOR THE YOUNG AND STRONG

iUniverse books may be ordered through booksellers or by contacting:

iUniverse
1663 Liberty Drive
Bloomington, IN 47403
www.iuniverse.com
1-800-Authors (1-800-288-4677)

ISBN: 978-1-4759-6767-8 (sc)
ISBN: 978-1-4759-6768-5 (ebk)

Printed in the United States of America

iUniverse rev. date: 01/23/2013

Dedicated to Pat and Caroline, Caroline's "A" Team, and the Deep Creek Families.

They taught us all we would ever need to know about courage, fortitude, friendship, and love.

God bless them all.

Table of Contents

Part III   Personal Adventures

Acknowledgments

I owe a debt of gratitude to the following individuals for their encouragement and support:

- Molly Pollasch, whose casual remark (mentioned in the Introduction) inspired me to write the book.

- Frank Sherwood, Bob Gerard, and Father Henry Haske, S.J. for allowing me to include their adventures in the chapter on adventurous friends. And two other friends: Pete Petersen and Paul Child, who, along with Frank Sherwood, submitted comprehensive essays on their adventures for the Appendix.

- Sandy Baumgartner, Executive Assistant to the Dean of the Richard J. Bolte, Sr. School of Business at Mount St. Mary's University, who provided the necessary skills I lacked to see the project through. Sandy makes the hard work look easy and encourages you in the process.

- Carol Herrmann, my daughter and my first and last editor on anything I write. Carol has a keen eye for problems of both content and writing. She was a terrific help with this book.

- My children: Mark, Carol, and Cathy; and their spouses: Gail, Cameron, and Fritz. All are always supportive of anything the family does. As always, their encouragement has meant a great deal to me.

- My grandchildren: John, Brian, Katie, Matthew, Patrick, Colleen, Kelly, and Caroline. A group with absolutely no downside. They are a constant source of love and inspiration.

- My wife, Pat: always a one-person cheering section for our family. She remains with us in spirit, always inspiring us to do our best. Her imprint is on this book as it was with earlier books. And that has improved it. God Bless!

Chapter 1

Introduction

We all occasionally have eye-opening experiences. I had one several years ago while at lunch with a friend, Molly Pollasch. She and I are both long-term cancer survivors, and an off-hand remark she made struck me: "You know, John, life has many adventures. When you are weakened by chemotherapy, even being able to venture forth to do your grocery shopping is an adventure."

That remark made me think. It opened my eyes to an entirely new way to view adventure—not as something rare and available only to a select few, but something available to us all, regardless of our circumstances, and something to enrich our lives.

The notion of being a lifelong adventurer began to haunt me and eventually led to this book: my attempt to share this idea, and perhaps impact some lives for the better.

Think for a moment. Are we not all intrigued by adventures, both real and fictional, that we encounter in books and on film? These are entertaining venues, and we should enjoy them. But too often we leave the reading and watching experiences with an unfortunately limited view of adventure: that it includes only intense physical activities and is available only to the young and strong. A very limited view, indeed.

History buffs can even succumb to the mindset that views adventure as largely in the past. Hasn't all the earth's landmass been explored and charted, its mountains climbed, its oceans crossed, its outer space explored? Yes, of course, much adventure has already occurred. But I've become convinced, like my friend, that for those with imagination, the opportunities for adventure are limitless.

I'd like to propose a new definition or criteria for adventure: It is the pursuit of any goal that may be beyond one's reach. It can be physical, emotional, intellectual, or even spiritual. But it always involves an individual pushing his or her limits, and it always carries the risk of failure. Physical goals can be risky to life and limb; intellectual goals can place one's reputation at risk; emotional and spiritual goals can lead to life-changing experiences where our happiness is at risk.

I wrote this book to give "you" the eye-opening experience of viewing adventure in this new way—to put you on a search for personal adventures to enrich your life.

My approach will be to literally fill your head with stories to help you see adventure's many dimensions. You will read of adventures that are physically demanding, of course. But you will also encounter examples of intellectual, emotional, and spiritual adventures. You will see these adventures through a group of diverse individuals, read of what they did, and often, through their own words, get clues to their motivations and the risks and rewards involved. And my goal is always to help you recognize the opportunities for adventure in your own life.

The diagram below (Roadmap of the Book) depicts the concept and content of the book.

Roadmap of the Book

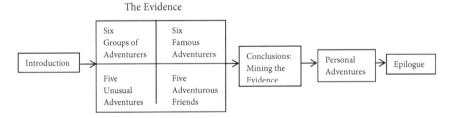

The heart of the book lies in "the evidence"—the stories of adventure. These are provided in four chapters, as follows:

<u>Six Groups of Adventurers</u>

- Astronauts
- Mountain Climbers
- Runners

- Writers
- Readers
- Travelers

Six Famous Adventurers

- Sir Ernest Shackleton—Explorer
- Amelia Earhart—Aviator
- Jackie Robinson—Athlete
- Martin Luther King, Jr.—Dreamer
- Pope John XXIII—Reformer
- Teddy Roosevelt—Ultimate Activist

Five Unusual Adventures

- Intellectual Adventure: A Return to the Great Books
- Planning Adventure: Climbing the Seven Summits
- Travel Adventure: Circling the Globe by Motorcycle
- Sea Adventure: A Late-life Racing Crew
- Spiritual Adventure: A Thirty Day Retreat

Five Adventurous Friends

- Dr. Frank P. Sherwood, Ph.D.
- Colonel Robert J. Gerard, Ph.D.
- Father Henry B. Haske, S.J.
- Colonel Peter B. Petersen, DBA
- Colonel Paul W. Child, Jr.

Following these stories I attempt to mine the evidence and form some conclusions. I then share a few experiences: past, and hopefully future, adventures of my own.

As you read these stories I think you will find what I have also discovered: These adventurers had a variety of motivations and some interesting personal characteristics in common. They all pushed boundaries. They all both learned and taught. And, most important of all, adventure added purpose, joy, and zest to their lives—as it can for you and me.

So, my question to you is this: Do you want a richer life bad enough to take some risks to achieve it? If so—read on. And act on what you discover!

Part I

The Evidence:
Stories of Adventure

Chapter 2

Six Groups of Adventurers

The groups of adventurers discussed in this chapter are:

- Astronauts
- Mountain Climbers
- Runners
- Writers
- Readers
- Travelers

These were picked from a large list of candidate groups. But they were not picked at random. Personal interest and experience played a role in selecting them. I've been a devoted runner, writer, reader, and traveler all my life. And astronauts and mountain climbers, the subjects of a rich body of literature, hold lessons not found elsewhere, and are simply too exciting to omit. So I'll begin with these two groups.

Astronauts

I decided early-on that I would include the Apollo astronauts as one of the groups. How could I not? Going to the moon is unarguably the greatest adventure ever. Thus, the motivations and reflections of the two dozen Apollo astronauts are important to getting at the heart of the adventuring spirit.

I found there was no shortage of information on the subject. One day I walked into my local Barnes and Noble bookstore and found a large table covered with books about the Apollo program. After examining them all and reading several, I found the perfect resource: *Voices from the Moon:*

Apollo Astronauts Describe Their Lunar Experiences, by Andrew Chaikin with Victoria Kohl.

This book was developed from over 150 hours of interviews with 23 of the 24 Apollo astronauts. The book includes a selection of quotations by the astronauts—"candid and deeply personal reflections." What I have tried to do here is mine their remarks for the experiences and motivations of these men who volunteered for and undertook these dangerous missions. Though admittedly fragmentary and out of context, these remarks provide important clues to what drove this group of adventurers.

Before reading the comments of the astronauts themselves, it may be helpful to see how the author, Chaikin, characterizes them:

"The men of Apollo were children during the early days of aviation, captivated by the exploits of Charles Lindbergh and the Flying Aces of World War I. They grew up to become jet pilots . . . and many ascended to the rarefied atmosphere of test flight . . . flying the hottest and most dangerous planes around. All were overachievers who wanted nothing more than to tackle a job almost no one else could accomplish. And so when the space age began and the word astronaut entered the language, it seemed as if this fantastic new enterprise had been made for them."

This view was validated by the comments so many made about their early life and their life goals and motivations. Let's look at a small collection of these comments.

> "[As a kid] I was thinking about guys who flew fighters in World War I. And I thought about the Lindberghs. I used to build paper airplane cockpits on the floor . . . and pretend I was flying, for hours—not space. But it's the flying that got me to the right place at the right time."
>
> Pete Conrad

> "I enjoy flying. That's all I wanted to do. When I was a little kid, I wanted to fly."
>
> Ken Mattingly

> "It came down to two words: higher and faster."
>
> Tom Stafford

"I had one goal—that was participating in the program and making sure the program was a success."

Frank Borman

"I don't focus on self-satisfaction, and being first, and those kinds of things . . . I take certain pleasures in the achievements, the technical achievements. And not just in an overall sense, but the little details here and there. Finding ways to accomplish the job."

Neil Armstrong

"It's my belief, no one could've participated in such an adventure without reinforcing your belief, in whatever belief you had before you left . . . In my case, it confirmed there is a God."

Ron Evans

"As far as returning to a normal life. I don't think any of us ever returned to normal life; I don't think any of us were normal people to start with."

Alan Shepard

"I've always said that the thing I did the best and enjoyed the most was getting there and getting back."

Pete Conrad

"It was a great experience that I had. It's one of those things that come along, not once in a lifetime, but once in a millennium, maybe."

Dick Gordon

This collection of comments points to a group of extraordinary men motivated mainly by the opportunity to practice their craft (flying) and extending that craft past all previous limits. There appears to be no thought of a life beyond this adventure, certainly no hint of using the space experience as a stepping stone to anything more lucrative or exciting.

Of course, as relatively young men, they did need post-Apollo employment. In a cover story in its July 27, 2009 issue, *Time* Magazine highlighted the

Apollo roles of each of the 24 and provided a brief sketch of each person's life after leaving the program. About half served as executives in industry and/or started their own technical consulting firms. Several became CEO's of major aerospace companies. Two were elected to Congress. But about half turned their attention to a wildly diverse collection of interests and experiences: religion, investing, restaurants, and real estate. The group includes five authors, a professor, and an artist—all pursuits of technical or personal interests, and seemingly devoid of any effort to capitalize on their Apollo experience beyond the joy and satisfaction of having participated. And, I think there is a reason for this: Nothing could ever match their experience. Astronaut Mike Collins said it best: "I have done things and been places you simply would not believe, and I keep that inside me."

What an adventure! What a group!

Mountain Climbers

I know, talking about this sport to ordinary people may seem a stretch—and it is. But I decided to include it for much the same reason I included astronauts, marathon runners, and others who do things beyond the capacity or even the imagination of most of us mortals. I included it simply because it *is* extreme—and sometimes we have to look at the extremes to find our answers. This is one of those situations. Perhaps these stories will convince you (as they have me) that mountain climbing is a metaphor for life, and that by immersing ourselves in the motivations of climbers we may gain the inspiration and motivation to figuratively climb our own mountains in search of our own unique adventures.

So, how can we get a handle on those who practice this extraordinary form of adventure? One thing I've found is that the elite practitioners of this art (and it is an art) like to write about their experiences. I became fascinated with the writings of these very articulate adventurers. And much of what I read gave me clues to their motivations.

One book, above all others, found late in my search, proved to be a goldmine of information, enabling me to say: I think I see it, finally!

The book is *Beyond Risk: Conversations With Climbers* by climber Nicholas O'Connell. The book provides a very brief history of mountaineering, including the many changes in objectives and technical developments that have characterized the sport over the past two hundred years: Tackling tougher climbs, with and without oxygen, pins, and other hardware;

climbing in massive expeditions with elaborate support systems; and going it alone in solo climbs. Quite a story in itself.

But more important for our purposes here is the author's focus on individual climbers. He conducted in-depth interviews with seventeen of the world's most innovative and accomplished climbers. After briefly outlining the achievements of each climber, he reports on his interviews, which were focused on a series of penetrating questions: What got them interested in climbing; how do they assemble resources; how do they cope with success, failure, and danger? And, the most important question of all, for our purposes: Why do they climb? And the amazing thing to me was the similarity of answers to the last question: their motivation for climbing.

Without attempting to recount the achievements of these elite climbers, let me just provide the names of a half dozen, and their verbatim responses to the question of concern here: Why do you participate in this extreme life-threatening sport?

> "Climbing is one of the center points of my life . . . I would not make a distinction between why I am living and why I am climbing. Climbing is a part of my life . . . a [way] to express what I know, what I feel, what I can do. I like to be creative."

> Reinhold Messner

> "The danger has been an attraction. The fear has been a stimulating factor. It's been quite an important part of why I've done it."

> Sir Edmund Hillary

> "Why do people need to go to the moon or underneath the sea? Before us, Odysseus wanted to go beyond his limits. Curiosity and fantasy brought man down from the trees, where he was an ape."

> Walter Bonatti

> "It's the physical satisfaction of feeling yourself climbing and then the sensual appreciation of the surroundings."

> Chris Bonington

"My climbs in the mountains are mystical experiences for me. And they are extremely positive. They make it easier to accept all the negative aspects of life—getting older, getting weaker, getting ill from time to time . . . . You experience in a short time what life is."

Voytek Kurtyka

"My life and climbing are so intertwined that they're one and the same. Climbing's my life and my life's climbing . . . I like the physical feeling. I like the emotional and mental challenge."

Jeff Lowe

In reading the mountain climbing literature, I found myself amazed at the enormity of the task and the similarity and simplicity of motivations for climbing. Though fame and fortune have indeed come to some elite climbers, that seems to be an accidental/incidental benefit. The joy and satisfaction of testing their limits drives most of them.

While reading about their adventures I found myself living vicariously through these brave souls. And while not capable to be one of them, I knew I would love to be among them, so rich is the life experience of the mountaineer.

Runners

I included this group because I was one of them for over 40 years. And though long ago my bad back forced me to switch to walking, I still think of myself as a runner.

My own running didn't really fit my present definition of adventurer. Aside from some competitive track and cross country in school, I ran mainly for fitness, the camaraderie of like-minded partners, and the opportunity to think undisturbed on the open road. Hardly adventure, but I relished every hour of it.

My starting theory for this piece was that running becomes an adventure when its primary purpose is to test our capabilities—to discover just how far we can push past pain and exhaustion to a place where we learn something important about ourselves. But I needed additional research to test that idea.

To test my theory I decided to search the running literature for the motivations of those who run marathons and ultramarathons. I found that there is an abundance of literature about such runners. They have lots of road time to think and an inclination to talk and write about their sport.

I settled on two sources, written some 25 years apart: A 1977 book, *The Boston Marathon* by Joe Falls; and a 2001 book, *To the Edge: A Man, Death Valley, and The Mystery of Endurance* by Kirk Johnson.

All traditional marathons are 26 miles and 385 yards long—somewhat over two hours of running by the winners. The most famous is the Boston Marathon, an annual event held on Patriots' Day (April 19th). The first such race was in 1897, and there has been a race every year since, except for 1918.

Ultramarathons can be any length greater than the standard marathon—but Johnson's narrative takes us to the Badwater Ultramarathon: A 135 mile footrace in mid-summer through Death Valley, from the lowest, hottest spot in the Western Hemisphere to Mt. Whitney, the highest point in the continental United States.

Joe Falls was a sports writer. His book describes the history of the Boston Marathon and tells the story of its legendary participants and winners. I was particularly interested in his observations and comments about the 99% of the participants who run the race with no hope of winning. My question was: Why do they do it?

Falls points out that there really was no prize associated with this race: at the time only a laurel wreath to the winner and some beef stew for all finishers. So, why pursue this? Why suffer through all the necessary training and the agony of this very demanding course? For the small group of possible winners there is the hope of a new record, or the notoriety from the press and sports magazines. These things may be a part of the motivation for the elite—but what about the thousands of participants who will trail behind them—by hours? Falls captures the essence of it all this way:

> "It's the people in the race (who) gather on that village green in Hopkinton to begin The Great Adventure. They hope to go the full distance and experience that sweet feeling of success, crossing the finish line. Maybe it's three o'clock. Maybe it's four o'clock. Maybe it's six o'clock and everyone has gone home. But if the Boston Marathon is

about anything at all, it is about finishing: to conquer one's self."

So winning has nothing to do with this adventure. It is irrelevant to nearly every one of the ordinary/extraordinary participants. Simply to finish, to survive, to conquer one's self—that's what this adventure is about.

Kirk Johnson's story of the ultramarathon is more personal. He was a 41 year old reporter for the *New York Times* with a family to which he was very committed. His older brother had committed suicide, and Johnson started running to escape and feel closer to his brother who had been a gifted athlete. His involvement with Badwater started with curiosity and ended with obsession. As he says, he had "written an article about Death Valley and its bizarre desert ultramarathon and then, through some error of cosmic miscasting, had fallen under its spell." As he tells the story of his research, particularly his personal interviews with participants, we can sense his ever-growing attraction to running this seemingly impossible race.

Johnson finally decided to run the race, taking a year off from work and committing himself to preparing for it. During this training he experienced a feeling of personal change: "I felt like a man without a country. I didn't belong to the only club that would fully understand me—the universe of ultramarathoners—and yet, by attempting to get there I was distancing myself, day by day, from the world in which I'd been a part."

Long story short: Johnson ran the race and finished it with the help of his support team (his sister and brother). Forty two runners started the race and nine dropped out. The winning time was 27 hours, 49 minutes. Johnson's time was 54 hours, 26 minutes. He finished last—but he finished!

The motivations of the runners? Who can say for sure? This is a quiet bunch. But we can learn something from Johnson's own experience, from his later reflections:

> "By moving, you find out how to move. By believing that
> an untapped source of strength exists, it becomes manifest.
> Act as though you are among the elect, and perhaps you
> will be . . . Search out the worst you can imagine and there
> you will find the best that is in you."

I ended my research feeling that my theory was validated: Distance running is about pushing yourself to the point where you learn something new and vitally important about yourself and your abilities. A noble goal—well worth the effort.

Writers

I must admit a bias: I'm in love with writing. I did only work-related writing until I was approaching retirement as a college professor ten years ago. But I always looked forward to the freedom of writing in retirement. I had some things I wanted to say. Plus, the notion of tackling self-imposed projects was appealing to me. I've written four books in retirement. So, I have a dog in this fight, and I want you in it with me. I want you to consider writing as one part of your life. Trust me, you can—and if you stay with me on this, you might be putting yourself on the path to a particularly rewarding intellectual adventure.

Let's begin by reading the comments of four of my favorite authors as they reflect on their craft:

- David McCullough
- Laura Hillenbrand
- David Halberstam
- Mary Higgins Clark

The historian, David McCullough, has written a number of biographies (e.g., *John Adams* and *Truman*) and also histories of events and projects (e.g., *The Great Bridge* and *The Johnstown Flood*). His statement in an interview on the TV program *Booknotes*, shows him to be partly motivated by curiosity—the urge to learn.

> "I feel that each project I've undertaken has been a huge adventure, a lesson in a world, a subject, a territory I knew nothing about. People will sometimes say to me, 'Well, what is your theme?' As I start on a new book I haven't the faintest idea. That's one of the reasons I'm writing the book."

And in a piece for the *Washington Post*, McCullough emphasizes both learning and telling as motivations.

> "I write to find out. There isn't anything in this world that isn't inherently interesting—if only someone will explain it to you in English, if only someone will frame it in a story."

Sometimes the author's motivation is to research an event in order to answer some haunting question. The recent book *Unbroken* by Laura Hillenbrand was so motivated. The book explores the life of Louis Zamperini, a distance runner who competed in the 1936 Olympics and later became an airman during World War II. After his plane crashed in the Pacific, he and another crewman survived 47 days in a raft at sea, only to be captured by the Japanese and subjected to unimaginable torture until the end of the war.

In an interview, Hillenbrand gives this reason for spending several years researching and writing this book: "It is a breathtaking story, but, for me, the question that informs it is equally involving. How do men survive the unsurvivable, physically and emotionally? I wrote the book to explore that question."

The distinguished journalist and historian, the late David Halberstam, wrote some twenty books on a wide range of subjects—most best sellers. His book, *The Best and the Brightest,* was a defining book on the Vietnam War. His final book, *The Coldest Winter,* is a monumental work on the Korean War, which has been somewhat neglected by historians.

In an interview on the TV program *Booknotes* about his book, *The Fifties,* Halberstam spoke of his attraction to the life of a writer:

> "It's a wonderful privileged life, you know, being a book writer. I live a good life, and I can have both my private life and my professional life. There's a wonderful level of privacy and a wonderful level of engagement in the society. I have the best of both worlds."

Finally, a comment from a writer of fiction—wonderful, exciting fiction— and lots of it: Mary Higgins Clark. In a piece for *The Washington Post* in 1999, she wrote:

> "Now, 25 years, 17 novels and 3 short story collections later, I'm still in love with what I do. Writing is essentially a solitary profession. It is: The idea that won't go away, the characters who start out as silhouettes and then take on flesh, the place, the season, the time span. It is: The excitement of setting out on a journey that will have unexpected twists and turns, unexpected land mines, a good deal of self-doubt, and a final sense of fulfillment."

In the comments of these famous authors we find many motivations: To learn something new; to share some knowledge, skill, or story; to enjoy a unique way of life, one characterized by hard work but also great personal freedom. These authors obviously love their craft. But how available is this intellectual adventure to most of us? More available than you might imagine.

Think for a moment about just one type of writing project. Think of a person with a life that would be interesting mainly to family. Imagine that person patiently setting down his or her story—perhaps enlisting the help of a son or granddaughter with a flair for writing and facility with computers. Imagine them turning out a manuscript that is reproduced, simply bound and given to each family member as a present. What an adventure such a project would be, and what a joy it would bring to many—including the writer.

If I now have your attention, and I hope I do, let me share a few personal thoughts—the product of writing four books in the past 12 years, two commercially published and two self-published.

I've spent 50 years as both a practicing manager and a teacher of leadership and management, and I used these books to crystallize my thinking about my experiences and to share some ideas—my bottom lines about what works in organizations.

But, the desire to share information is only part of my motivation. As I've said, I'm retired, and I like having a project—actually I need one. And writing is a challenging adventure that I've grown to love. It forces me to set a personal goal and follow through to achieve it. It is an exercise in planning, researching, organizing material—and buckling down to the work of making my own schedule to see the job through. It is not all joy. I often suffer from writer's block or simply get weary of the hard work. But the reward of a finished project has always been worth the demands of the process.

Patience! I'm almost at the end of my campaign to encourage you to write. But I must address one more issue—perhaps the obstacle that discourages most people from writing: finding a publisher. Not to worry—you don't need one. Simply investigate the many approaches to self-publishing.

I've written books under contract to both small and large publishing houses, and I have also self-published two books. My bottom line advice is: Never, never, seek a contract with a commercial publisher unless you need the money or need the book as a professional credential. If your primary goal is to experience the adventure of writing your story, always opt for the freedom afforded by self-publishing. The cost today is minimal, the product is of equal professional quality, and, most important, you can write what you want, the way you want, without the annoying and time-consuming interference inherent in commercial publishing.

So what's stopping you? Start now—WRITE!!

Readers

It's hard to crawl into another person's head to find what really motivates some to be serious readers. But occasionally we get a clue from someone who reveals herself—totally. Such a person is Nancy Pearl, who has spent her life as a librarian, bookseller, and, yes, reader. Currently the Director of Library Programming at the Washington Center for the Book at the Seattle Public Library, Nancy has written three books as guides to reading. One of her books, *Book Lust: Recommended Reading for Every Mood, Moment, and Reason* contains this passage which says all we could ever need to know about her motivation:

> "Reading has always brought me pure joy. I read to encounter pure joy. I read to encounter new worlds and new ways of looking at our own world. I read to enlarge my horizons, to gain wisdom, to experience beauty, to understand myself better, and for the pure wonderment of it all. I read to marvel over how writers use language in ways I never thought of. I read for company, and for escape. Because I am incurably interested in the lives of other people, both friends and strangers, I read to meet myriad folks and to enter their lives—for me, a way of vanquishing the otherness we all experience."

She concludes her introduction with an interesting quotation from an essay, *How Should One Read a Book?* by Virginia Woolf:

> "I have sometimes dreamt . . . that when the Day of Judgment dawns and the great conquerors and lawyers and statesmen come to receive their rewards . . . . The Almighty will turn to Peter and will say . . . . When he sees us coming with our books under our arms, 'Look, these

need no reward. We have nothing to give them here. They have loved reading.'"

Another even more revealing source originates in a small but increasingly influential bookstore in Madison, Connecticut: R.J. Julia Booksellers. The bookstore hosts over two hundred author events each year; and it won the *Publishers Weekly* Booksellers of the Year Award in 1995. Its founder, Roxanne J. Coady, coedited (with Joy Johannessen) a small book that is a treasure trove for anyone interested in why people read: *The Book That Changed My Life: 71 Remarkable Writers Celebrate the Books That Matter Most to Them.*

Each of the 71 authors had been a guest speaker at the bookstore, and each contributed a page or two on his or her favorite book or books. The resulting list of favorite books by the authors, many of whom are quite famous, should be in itself of interest to devoted readers seeking suggested titles. But for our purposes here, what is most interesting is what these short personal essays reveal about motivators to read.

The 71 authors each named the book that most changed their lives, then described the book's impact on them. I've selected ten brief comments from the 71 essays that I think show the potential impact of books on readers—and give us subtle clues on how reading can change lives.

- Nicholas A. Basbanes on *The Works of Shakespeare*

  "I was totally dazzled by the imagery, the poetry, the insights Shakespeare offered into the frailties of human nature."

- Graeme Base on *The Lord of the Rings*

  "The book that changed my life? What had changed in me? Simply put, I finally got it: A book could do more than help you pass an exam, it could lift you up and sweep you away, and I liked the feeling."

- Jeff Benedict on *The Little Engine That Could*

  "My confidence to try new things and be unafraid of failure began with a simple children's book."

- Robert Kurson on *The Denial of Death*

  "In it, I find answers to nearly every question I can think to ask about being human and about being in the world."

- Margot Livesey on *Jane Eyre*

  "The book did show me that life is change. Like Jane, my life had changed for the worse, and like hers, it could also change for the better. Time would, irrevocably, carry me to a new place."

  "Jane Eyre speaks to the secret, vulnerable part of ourselves that has little to do with age or gender or race or situation."

- Anne Perry on *The Man Who Was Thursday*

  "*The Man Who Was Thursday* is vast and wise, filled with words and ideas that make sense of pain and loneliness and the length of the whole journey of life."

- Brother Christopher on *The Seven Story Mountain*

  "Merton's journey charted a path into my own heart, stirring questions I did not dare ignore. *The Seven Story Mountain* had awakened a primal desire that would henceforth be a factor in every decision I would ever make, in every moment of self-discovery I would ever experience."

- Maureen Corrigan on *David Copperfield*

  "Reading *David Copperfield* that first time at age thirteen fired my resolve to find work that would be satisfying in some way and draw upon whatever gifts I had."

- David Halberstam on *The Reason Why*

  "It was my introduction to what you might call the glitches of history, that is, all the things they don't tell you in high school history classes."

- Frank Rich on *Act One*

> "*Act One* showed me a way out of my childhood. If Moss
> Hart could escape his circumstance through hard work,
> luck, the kindness of strangers, and the sheer force of his
> passion, maybe I could too."

So . . . what does it all mean? What do the above comments tell us about
reading as an adventure? In her book's introduction, Roxanne Coady
captures well the essence of the adventure of reading.

> "Every day in the store we see how books change lives, in
> big ways and small, from the simple desire to spend a few
> quiet hours in a comfy chair, swept away by a story, to the
> profound realization that the reader is not alone in the
> world, that there is someone else like him or her, someone
> who has faced the same fears, the same confusions, the
> same grief, the same joys. Reading is a way to live more
> lives, to experience more worlds, to meet people we care
> about and want to know more about, to understand others
> and develop compassion for what they confront and
> endure. It is a way to learn how to knit or build a house
> or solve an equation, a way to be moved to laughter and
> wonder and to learn how to live."

Bottom line: Reading is indeed an adventure—an intellectual one—and
often life-changing.

Travelers

Travelers, as a group, deserve a place in any collection of adventurers.
And you probably need no convincing about this because travel is such
a universal experience. Whether occasioned by a work transfer or by a
personal urge to go, to see, to be somewhere else—it is always an adventure
because in venturing out of our normal environment, we experience new
demands, thus stretching our capacity.

Travel requires us to cope with strange locations; new people; sometimes
markedly different cultures; and normally, increased physical demands.
And, think about it. For any one of these reasons we sometimes opt for the
security of the status quo and pass on travel opportunities.

But whenever we chose to go, to step out of our comfort zone and venture into the unknown, we become adventurers. Because what awaits us is some combination of excitement, danger, fun, sometimes even pain—but inevitably, a feeling of accomplishment. We risk something with an uncertain outcome. That makes our travel an adventure—a source of pride, joy, and fulfillment.

Chapter 3

Six Famous Adventurers

The adventurers discussed in this chapter are:

- Sir Ernest Shackleton—Explorer
- Amelia Earhart—Aviator
- Jackie Robinson—Athlete
- Martin Luther King, Jr.—Dreamer
- Pope John XXIII—Reformer
- Teddy Roosevelt—Ultimate Activist

With so many famous individuals to pick from, why go with these six? Both the magnitude and diversity in their collective achievements guided the selection. I wanted an explorer who had led expeditions, which pointed me to Shackleton and his achievements in Antarctica. It also seemed important to include a woman of high achievement in dangerous circumstances who not only broke new ground in her craft, but also prepared the world for women's achievements to come. The pioneer aviator Amelia Earhart seemed the perfect choice. Jackie Robinson was picked for advancing the cause of racial equality in athletics, and Martin Luther King, Jr. for his leadership in the Civil Rights Movement. Pope John XXIII may not be as well-known as the others, but his achievement in the early 1960s in surmounting fierce opposition to bring about reforms in his Church earned him his place on the list. As for Teddy Roosevelt—when you're searching for the ultimate activist in just about every phase of life and work, Roosevelt is the "must pick."

Researching the lives and deeds of these six adventurers was inspiring for me—and I hope the brief sketches that follow will similarly inspire you.

Sir Ernest Shackleton—Explorer

In searching for an explorer for this collection of adventurers, I turned to a favorite subject of mine: Sir Ernest Shackleton—possibly the best model ever of a small unit leader in search of adventure.

Shackleton (1874-1922) was an Irish explorer famous for his Antarctic expeditions. He accompanied Captain Robert Scott of the British Navy on the first inland exploration of Antarctica from 1901 to 1904, a failed effort to reach the South Pole. Then in 1907, Shackleton mounted his own expedition which came within 100 nautical miles of the South Pole. This was the closest anyone had gotten to the Pole, and for that achievement Shackleton was knighted.

The expedition for which Shackleton is most famous was an unsuccessful venture, but a spectacular leadership achievement. Briefly, Shackleton led a party of 28 men into the Waddell Sea in December 1914, in an effort to cross the Antarctic. Ice crushed his ship, *Endurance*. His party escaped in three small boats to Elephant Island. Then, in a small boat, he and five companions made a daring 800-mile journey to South Georgia Island and crossed its glacier-covered mountainous ridge to find help in successfully rescuing the 23 men he'd left behind on Elephant Island on May 20, 1916, after 17 months of inconceivable hardship and danger. All 23 men were rescued. Shackleton did not lose a single man throughout this journey.

A few memorable quotations illustrate the respect he earned from contemporaries and comrades:

- Roald Amundsen, the Norwegian explorer who was first to reach the South Pole, paid this tribute to Shackleton:

   "Courage and willpower can make miracles. I know of no better example than what that man has accomplished."

- British explorer Apsley Cherry-Garrard compared Shackleton to others in this statement:

   "For a joint scientific and geographical piece of organization, give me Scott; for a winter journey, give me Wilson; for a dash to the pole and nothing else, Amundsen; and if I am in the devil of a hole and want to get out of it, give me Shackleton every time."

- Frank Worsley, Captain of the *Endurance*, wrote in his own book, *Endurance*:

> "And what of him as a man? I recalled the way in which he had led his party across the ice-floes after the *Endurance* had been lost; how by his genius for leadership he had kept us all in health; how by the sheer force of his personality he had kept our spirits up; and how, by his magnificent example, he had enabled us to win through when the dice of the elements were loaded heavily against us."

Those tributes were echoed by the members of his crew in their diaries and in countless books, articles, and talks given for years after the expedition.

During World War I, Shackleton was unable to serve in the military because of his age and a bad heart. But he served in a variety of diplomatic missions—and in 1921 acquired a converted Norwegian Sealer, renamed *Quest*, for still another expedition. He died of a heart attack on that voyage.

So, why did he do it? What drove Shackleton to these dangerous expeditions? As with many of the subjects in this book, it is hard to say. But in Shackleton's case some clues are given by statements he made and literature he loved.

In a statement on his view of life he wrote:

> "Some people say it is wrong to regard life as a game. I don't think so. Life means to me the greatest of all games."

And an extension of this thought is found in his motto: "Prospice" which means "look forward." It was the title of a Robert Browning poem he loved, which said in part:

> *No! Let me taste the whole of it, fare like my peers the heroes of old. Bear the brunt, in a minute pay life's glad arrears of pain, darkness and cold.*

But, maybe the bottom line on Shackleton's motivation is found in his own simple statement: "There is a peculiar fascination about going . . . I don't think I can explain it in words. But there's an excitement, a thrill—a sort of magnetic attraction about Polar exploration."

And why would it even be important to know Shackleton's motivation—important to us ordinary mortals who will never undertake such missions?

It's important because in Shackleton we have perhaps a model that gives us some glimpse of the adventurous spirit deep within us all—and thus might prod us into action in pursuit of our own unique adventures.

Amelia Earhart—Aviator

Amelia Earhart was an aviation pioneer. Her life was short, but full of adventure. Born in 1898, she died in 1937 while attempting the first round-the-world flight via the equator.

Considered the foremost woman aviator, her list of flying achievements is daunting:

- In 1918, two years after she made her first solo flight, she set a women's altitude record of 14,000 feet.

- She was the second person, after Lindbergh, to complete a solo flight across the Atlantic.

- She was the first person to fly from Hawaii to the coast of the United States.

Earhart was a true activist—interested and engaged in many pursuits: She co-founded an airline, wrote books, consulted on scientific and aviation matters—and, in the process, opened career doors for other women.

She died pursuing a life-long goal: to circumnavigate the globe by air. She and a colleague, Fred Noonan, set off from Miami on June 1, 1937. The first legs of their historic trip through South America, Africa, India, and Australia were uneventful. But on July 1st they left New Guinea on a leg requiring them to cross 2,500 miles of open ocean. She never revealed her exact position on this flight, but, in her last message, informed the Coast Guard Cutter *Itasca* that she had only a half hour's gas left and that no land was in sight. When her plane did not arrive at its destination, the *Itasca* conducted a search, but no trace of Earhart, Noonan, or their plane was ever found. To this day, her disappearance remains a mystery.

However, Earhart's motivation for all that she achieved is clear. The title of her autobiography, *The Fun of It*, says it all. Others in similar pursuits may have sought money or fame. But for Earhart, though she clearly relished her fame, fun was her primary driver—and for that reason I consider her the quintessential adventurer.

Jackie Robinson—Athlete

Jackie Robinson was the first black athlete to play baseball in the major leagues. His extraordinary journey through the racial prejudices of the time to baseball's Hall of Fame must qualify as one of the greatest achievements in sport—and an extraordinary personal adventure.

Robinson's record in baseball is a testament to his athletic ability. He joined the Brooklyn Dodgers in 1947 at the age of 28. In his first season he hit .297, scored 125 runs, led the league in stolen bases (29), and as the Dodgers won its first pennant since 1941, was named Rookie of the Year. He subsequently led his team to six World Series in 10 years. In 1949 he was named the league's Most Valuable Player, leading the league in batting (.342) and stolen bases (37) while scoring 122 runs, and batting in 124 runs.

But to see Robinson's achievement for what it was in a larger sense—a true adventure of body, mind, and spirit—we need an appreciation of the racial bigotry of the times, and the courage it took to face that bigotry.

Robinson's first taste of what the future would hold came during an interview with Branch Rickey, General Manager of the Dodgers, who had the nerve to hire him. Rickey described every possible obstacle Robinson would, and ultimately did, face: bigotry, vocal slurs from both fans and teammates, intentional beanballing by pitchers and spiking by opposing players. Rickey said, to be a successful experiment paving the way for other black players, Robinson would have to accept the abuse: "I'm looking for a ballplayer with guts enough not to fight back. They'll taunt you, goad you. Anything to make you fight. Anything to bring about a race riot in the ball park. If they succeed, they'll be able to prove that having a Negro in baseball doesn't work."

Rickey was on an adventure of his own: to bring the first black player into the major leagues. But it was Jackie Robinson that made it work. He accepted the challenge, stepped into the unknown, and found it every bit as difficult as Rickey had anticipated. But in the end he prevailed mightily, and his adventure earned him the respect of the whole nation and changed his sport forever, and for the good.

Martin Luther King, Jr.—Dreamer

Martin Luther King, Jr. was born in Georgia in 1929. So he grew up in a time and place of great racial inequality and tension. "Jim Crow" laws in the South barred blacks from white-only schools and just about every other public facility. Literacy tests, pole taxes, and obscure "grandfather clauses" (excluding anyone whose grandfather had not voted) prevented most blacks from voting.

But three events at mid-century signaled that change was in the air: In 1948 President Truman integrated the armed forces; in 1954 the US Supreme Court handed down a decision that made desegregation of schools the law of the land; and on December 1, 1955, a brave black woman (Rosa Parks) refused to move to the rear of a bus in Montgomery, Alabama and was arrested. The Rosa Parks incident did three things: It caused a year-long boycott by Montgomery's black citizens and ultimately the desegregation of Montgomery buses; it brought civil rights to the attention of the whole country; and it gave rise to a new civil rights leader, Martin Luther King, Jr., a young pastor who was asked to serve as president of the organization formed to run the boycott.

King was a remarkable leader. He was inspired by the leadership model of India's greatest leader, Mahatma Gandhi: nonviolent disobedience. In his first speech to his colleagues, King struck a chord that guided all his subsequent actions through his years of civil rights leadership:

> "First and foremost, we are all American citizens . . . we are
> not here to advocate violence . . . the only weapon we have
> is the weapon of protest . . . . the great glory of American
> democracy is the right to protest for right."

For over a dozen years King was the central figure in the civil rights struggle. His life was threatened constantly as he led his movement—and predictably, he lost his life to an assassin's bullet in 1968.

King's adventure was ambitious: to change his nation's attitudes and laws oppressing blacks. And largely through his actions those laws did change. At the same time it must be acknowledged that racial discrimination has not ended. It still exists in subtle forms in many parts of the country, but one only need look at the present occupant of the White House to realize the remarkable progress made—progress that King started.

King's story bears all the elements of adventure: danger, hardship, uncertainty. So why did he embark on this adventure? Simple. Martin Luther King, Jr. had a dream, never expressed more clearly than in his "I Have a Dream" speech in Washington, DC in 1963, which said in part:

"I have a dream that one day this nation will rise up and live out the true meaning of its creed . . . that all men are created equal."

And so it was: an adventure powered by a dream!

Pope John XXIII—Reformer

Pope John XXIII was elected Pope in 1958 at the age of 76. Because of his age there was no expectation that he would rock the boat in a Church that had changed little in hundreds of years. But the new Pope fooled them all. He turned out to be the successful proponent of radical change in an effort to modernize his Church.

The change was accomplished through the vehicle of The Second Vatican Council (Vatican II): a meeting of the 3000 Bishops of the Church from around the world. Vatican II was convened in October 1962. It was only the twentieth such gathering in 2000 years, the first since 1869, and only the second since the Council of Trent in 1545.

So, convening Vatican II was an event of great importance—and the resulting changes in the Church can only be regarded as revolutionary: It reshaped the Church and its relations with other religions of the world, changed the liturgy of the Mass, gave local bishops and the laity expanded roles in church functions and leadership, and went far to heal divisions between Catholics and non-Catholics.

You might wonder: Why such an elaborate process? Can't the Pope just order the changes he wants? Well, yes he can, but that was not the way of Pope John XXIII. A man of exceptional organizational skills, he wanted to pull the changes through the system to better legitimize and institutionalize those changes. Convening the Council changed the whole nature of the effort: the difficulty, opposition, risk involved, and the uncertainty of the outcome. And that is exactly why it fits our definition of an adventure.

So, what was the Pope's motivation? Why fight this battle? Two reasons: John XXIII personally felt that there were elements of Church doctrine and policies that needed reexamination and updating. Plus, he recognized that Catholics at that time (17 years after the end of World War II) were becoming increasingly well-educated and informed. They would be raising questions and concerns and not be satisfied with the simple answer: because we said so.

Thus was born an adventure in institutional change and reform, by a leader ready and willing to brave the difficulties to make it happen.

Teddy Roosevelt—Ultimate Activist

In his biography of Roosevelt, Edmund Morris captured the many facets of Roosevelt's remarkable life and talents with this litany:

> "A Nobel Prize winner, a physical culturist, a naval historian, a biographer, an essayist, a paleontologist, a taxidermist, an ornithologist, a field naturalist, a conservationist, a big-game hunter, an editor, a critic, a ranchman, an orator, a country squire, a civil service reformer, a socialite, a patron of the arts, a colonel of cavalry, a former Governor of New York, the ranking expert on big-game mammals in North America, and the President of the United States."

I'll leave the recounting of his deeds as President to others, except to say that he was probably the most activist President in our history, which would be enough adventure for most men—but not for TR.

Sickly as a child, he pursued a lifetime of strenuous physical training and activity. Gifted with exceptional intellect, he engaged in lifelong learning through both travel and reading (1-3 books per day), and as an intellectual activist he wrote some 40 books. TR was the first President to ride in an automobile, submerge in a submarine, fly in an airplane, and travel outside the country.

Sorrow was also a constant in his life—and his reaction was adventure. When his beloved father died while TR was in college, he fled to the Maine woods to grieve through strenuous outdoor activities. When his first wife died he fled to the Badlands of North Dakota, where he lived as a rancher among outlaws. When his 1912 split with his party resulted in the election of Woodrow Wilson, he set out to explore the River of Doubt in Brazil, went big-game hunting, and chronicled his exploits.

And why did he do all this? His own words give us a clue. After his first wife died he wrote a friend: "It was a grim and evil fate, but I never believed it did any good to flinch or yield to any blow, nor does it lighten the blow to cease from working."

After his son Quentin was killed in World War I, TR wrote this tribute to him:

"Only those are fit to live who do not fear to die, and none are fit to die who have shrunk from the joys of life and the duty of life. Both life and death are part of the same great adventure."

Looking at the whole astounding range of his activities, I would say some were motivated by raw ambition, some served to blot out personal pain, but many were undertaken simply to satisfy a restless nature and an abundance of curiosity. But whatever the motivations, TR's life was indeed one great adventure.

Chapter 4

Five Unusual Adventures

The adventures discussed in this chapter are:

- Intellectual Adventure: A Return to the Great Books

- Planning Adventure: Climbing the Seven Summits

- Travel Adventure: Circling the Globe by Motorcycle

- Sea Adventure: A Late-life Racing Crew

- Spiritual Adventure: A Thirty Day Retreat

The picks here were easy. I was looking for the unusual, and found it on my bookshelves—five books acquired over the years describing these adventures. Read on, and you will encounter:

- A forty-eight year old successful film critic who decided to return to Columbia University to retake the Great Books courses he'd taken as a freshman.

- Two wealthy, fiftyish, business executives who decided to climb the highest mountain on each of the seven continents.

- A successful investor who circled the globe by motorcycle in search of adventure, learning, and investment opportunities.

- A senior citizen who, because of age, was excluded from participation in a sailing race to Hawaii—but ignored the rejection, formed his own crew of senior citizens, and completed the race.

- A college professor who, in search of deeper spirituality and life perspective, undertook a thirty day silent religious retreat.

When I first read their stories, I was filled with admiration for these unusual adventurers, a bit envious of them, and determined to seek a more exciting life for myself. I offer their stories here in hopes they might inspire you as well.

Intellectual Adventure: A Return to the Great Books

David Denby, a film critic, decided at the age of 48 to return to Columbia University and retake its two famous courses in Western classics that he had been required to take as a freshman. The courses (Literature Humanities and Contemporary Civilization) exposed the student to a wide range of authors (e.g., Homer, Plato, Augustine, Austen, Marx, Neitzsche), and hence they were sometimes referred to as the "Great Books" courses.

Denby decided not just to take the courses, but to write a book, entitled *Great Books*, about the experience. He had a number of motivations. He wanted to again experience life in the classroom—its atmosphere, teaching approaches, and the attitudes of very diverse, media-age students to these books. He also wanted to personally judge the relevance of these courses today. But, as I read his book, it became clear that Denby was driven, most of all, by the intense desire to again experience these books—to grapple with their ideas, from the viewpoint of a man with worldly knowledge and life experience. *Great Books* provides a wonderful overview of the content of the courses—the messages of the books themselves. It also treats the reader to a glimpse into college life, contemporary student attitudes, and insights into the ever ongoing academic and political debates about the value and suitability of such courses. But for our purposes here, perhaps the book's greatest value is that it depicts Denby's intellectual adventure as a journey of self-discovery.

In Denby's book we see all the components of his adventure: His reaction to seeing the books in the bookstore ("I was thrilled by the possibility that they might be difficult. I would read; I would study; I would sit with teenagers."); his terror at confronting his first examination; his growing respect and affection for so many of his teachers and fellow students; and his take on old ideas encountered anew.

In the end, we can see that Denby clearly enjoyed his experience. He found it extremely demanding but equally rewarding from a personal standpoint. His judgment of the courses is that they are the "most radical courses in the undergraduate curriculum." But he considers them important and valuable to all students of all backgrounds because: "These books speak most powerfully of what a human being can be. They dramatize the utmost man is capable of in love, suffering, and knowledge." Further, he concludes that reading and discussing the books is particularly relevant to today's young people because it "scrapes away the media haze of second handedness."

Denby's experience was a true intellectual adventure. He put his life on hold for an extended period, stepped out of his comfort zone, and found his new environment to be both a personal testing place and a place of profound learning.

Planning Adventure: Climbing the Seven Summits

Talk about an adventure that stretches you! This is one for the books—and yes, it is recorded in a book: *Seven Summits*.

This is the story of how two highly successful businessmen (Frank Wells and Dick Bass) in their early 50s and with little mountain climbing experience, shared a dream and pulled it off: They climbed the highest mountain on each of the world's seven continents (Aconcagua in South America; Mount Everest in Asia; Kilimanjaro in Africa; Vinson Massif in Antarctica; Mount McKinley in North America; Elbrus in Europe; and Mount Kosciusko in Australia).

This was a mountain climbing feat that had never been accomplished before. So who were these men and what attracted them to such a project? When the project was undertaken, in the early 1980s, Frank was President of Warner Brothers Studios and Dick was an entrepreneur with oil and ranching interests in Texas, the Snowbird Ski Resort in Utah, and coal interests in Alaska. Two wealthy, happily married men, living very comfortable lives. So why risk their lives on this daring, seemingly impossible enterprise?

To get at the question of why, it is necessary to understand the nature and magnitude of their task. First of all, there was the physical task of climbing these tough mountains: the skills and strength required and the harsh environments to be endured at altitude in places like the Arctic Circle and Antarctica. Second, each expedition would require extensive planning to assemble the necessary logistical support. Third, the location of some climbs would require confronting some political obstacles in obtaining the necessary permissions. Finally, these two men had heavy responsibilities in their personal and work worlds. They couldn't just walk away from all other obligations to train and climb.

Through their book, I traced the course of this fascinating adventure, from their earliest meetings and conversations, through the challenges confronted in each climb, to the final elaborate celebration of success four years later. I have to admit that it helped that they were wealthy. This was a costly enterprise, but for them, money was apparently never an issue. However, no one could "buy" success for such a project. Success had to be earned. But these two men had no need to seek success through such a project; they were already highly successful.

So what was the draw, the motivation? I have concluded that these were two guys who could not say no to what, for most of us, would seem an impossible dream. They had done the impossible all their lives, and just could not conceive of anything they couldn't do, or any obstacle they could not surmount.

For me, Dick Bass captured it all—the motivation, the source of confidence, and the joy of achievement—with Robert Service's poem, *The Rolling Stone*, which he recited for his comrades around a campfire on Kilimanjaro:

> To scorn all strife, and to view all life
>
> > With the curious eyes of a child;
>
> From the plangent sea to the prairie,
>
> > From the slum to the heart of the Wild.
>
> From the red-rimmed star to the speck of sand,
>
> > From the vast to the greatly small;
>
> For I know that the whole for the good is planned,
>
> > And I want to see it all.

And where better to see it all than from the tops of the world? So they just did it!

Travel Adventure: Circling the Globe by Motorcycle

Jim Rogers is a famous investor. In the 1970s he made what he described as "more money than I knew existed in the world." That money bought him more than possessions or a life of luxury. It bought him a much greater gift: freedom. And Rogers took it. At age 37 he retired and embarked on the adventure of a lifetime.

One of his passions was motorcycling; another was travel. And he had always had an urge to take a trip around the world, by motorcycle. Together with his girlfriend he set out to do just that. Just the two of them, on two motorcycles loaded with a carefully planned cargo of clothing and supplies.

In his book, *Investment Biker*, Rogers recounts what can only be described as a fantastic experience. On this trip of twenty-two months they drove 65,067 miles on land and traveled thousands more by sea, air, and railroad links across six continents—setting a world record for land travel. They not only circumnavigated the globe from east to west, but from north to south as well: from Johannesburg through North America to London; and from the southern tip of South America to Anchorage, Alaska. And the book describes the myriad problems on the way: Bad roads, bad weather, and some dangerous people; mechanical breakdowns and supply problems; and the ever present administrative hassles regarding border crossings.

Further, they did not just travel through these many great countries. They met and talked with all kinds of people: government officials, business owners, bankers, investors, and ordinary citizens.

So why did they do it? Why, in Rogers' case, with more money than he could ever need, would he embark on such a demanding journey, and with a very young (early twenties), inexperienced companion? Well, I've read his book and heard him talk about the trip. For Rogers, investing isn't just about making money. It is an exciting game, an adventure in its own right.

One of Rogers' objectives was to learn about the world and about investment opportunities that only personal observation could identify. And he certainly accomplished that. The book describes many of his conclusions and subsequent investment decisions.

As for Tabitha Estacrook, his girlfriend, I think the excitement of such a trip was a big draw, as was learning. On return she began a graduate program in international relations. On that Rogers commented: "She might be better equipped to teach it than someone who's only read about it in books."

Rogers has continued to be an active investor and nationally known commentator on international economic issues. He even took another trip around the world by car, and today he and his family reside in China where he continues his involvement in economic matters.

Finally, when I step back and view their amazing trip, I have to conclude that they went because they had to. Yes, there were learning and investment goals. But this was high adventure at its best. In the last lines of *Investment Biker*, I feel Rogers confirms this: "I've also learned that if you've got a dream, you have to try it; you must get it out of your system. You will never get another chance. If you want to change your life, do it."

Great advice!!

Sea Adventure: A Late-life Racing Crew

Dr. Gordon Livingston, MD recounts a great story of adventure in his book: *And Never Stop Dancing*.

The story begins in 2003, when a seventy year old man, Lloyd Sellinger, applies for a crew position in the Biennial Transpac Race from Los Angeles to Honolulu. Turned down because of his age, Lloyd decided to prepare his own 40-foot sailboat for the 2005 race, and staff it with crew members who were all over 65. Talk about revenge!

Livingston, who "had sailed nothing larger than thirty feet and had never been out of sight of land in a sailboat" applied and was accepted for membership in the crew that named itself "The Dirty Half Dozen." Other crewmembers included: A general contractor/engineer; an optometrist; a communications relay installer; and a member of the 1956 Hungarian Olympic Team—all experienced sailors.

Livingston tells the story of the training and crew camaraderie on the 2500-mile race. No, they did not win, far from it—but this motley crew of men over 65 did finish, and proudly.

Livingston's commentary on the finish touched me deeply:

"As we drew abreast of Oahu the sun rose behind us and bathed Diamond Head in the pristine glow of a new day. With the old Eagles barn burner, *Already Gone*, playing on the iPod, the years slipped away, and for a moment it was possible to feel the strength of our younger selves. We finished more than two days behind the first boat in our class; we suffered from a failure of speed but not of the heart or of the spirit. We were, finally, six old men on an old boat racing toward the embrace of those who loved us and in whose eyes we were already heroes."

And—what did they learn? Livingston captures the essence this way:

"A race across the Pacific in the twilight of life is a compelling metaphor for how to best confront the western horizon—flat out, spinnaker drawing, dolphins leaping alongside, in the company of kindred spirits. What could be better than this?"

The story of The Dirty Half Dozen left me inspired and just a bit envious.

Spiritual Adventure: A Thirty Day Retreat

This is the story of Paul Mariani, an author and college professor, who undertook a very demanding 30 day silent religious retreat. His purpose was to use the experience to gain perspective in many aspects of his life. He shares his experience with us in his book: *Thirty Days: On Retreat with the Exercises of St. Ignatius.*

Hold on a minute! I know some readers might raise an eyebrow on this one. Is it some kind of pitch for the Catholic Church? The answer is a clear NO. In the spirit of self-disclosure, I acknowledge that I am a practicing Catholic. And for that reason I considered rejecting this story for the book. But in the end, given the purpose of the book, I decided this story was too compelling to omit. Because, whatever our belief or disbelief in any form of religion, none of us can escape the curiosity of wondering: What's it all about?—this existence of ours. That puts all of us on some sort of spiritual journey, thus making another's journey relevant to us.

So, what was the adventure about? What are the Exercises of St. Ignatius? Sufficient for our purpose here is to know that the Exercises are a process designed by Ignatius, the founder of the Jesuit Order, nearly 500 years ago. Ignatius was a soldier who was led to a religious life after being seriously wounded. His spiritual search led him to the conclusion that it is important to look for God in the stuff of our everyday experiences, and that the key task in life is to discern our role in God's plan.

The process of this discernment, the silent 30 day Ignatian Retreat, has been practiced in the Jesuit Order through the years—every Jesuit must undertake it twice. But countless lay people have experienced the retreat as a spiritual adventure addressing many life issues—for example:

- How do I know what I am supposed to do in life?
- How do I make good decisions?
- How can I be happy?
- How can I face suffering?
- How do I love?

So . . . this retreat is aimed not just at religious matters, but at all the important issues in one's life.

Through his book, Mariani shares his experience with us. With clarity, humility, and uncommon candor he reports his actions and thoughts day-by-day. We literally travel with him through the thirty days—listen to him confront his past, and emerge with a feeling "that no matter how small we may think we are against the background of eternity, we do count in the cosmic scheme of things"—and with a "heightened sense of what it truly means to put others before ourselves."

In my view, Mariani set out on a profound adventure of the spirit—and one need not be a Christian, or even believe in God, to appreciate that adventure.

Chapter 5

Five Adventurous Friends

Through the process of researching adventures for this book, I've discovered that I have a lot of friends who meet my definition of adventurers.

In this chapter I'll introduce you to five such friends—selected from dozens I could have included. I'll briefly describe the adventures of three of them, then let three of them speak for themselves in longer pieces they wrote for the Appendix (Personal Stories of Three Adventurous Friends).

Dr. Frank P. Sherwood, Ph.D.

I first met Frank in 1976, when I enrolled in the doctoral program in public administration offered by The University of Southern California (USC) at its Washington Public Affairs Center (WPAC) in Washington, DC. Frank was the Founding Director of the program, taught some of my classes, and was research director for my dissertation. This early contact developed into a life-long friendship.

Frank's list of professional accomplishments is long and distinguished. An abbreviated list here should make that point: Youngest director of USC's Public Administration Program; Founding Director of the Federal Executive Institute (FEI); Founding Director of the WPAC; head of the public administration program at Florida State University; and a long-term management consultant to Iran, Brazil and numerous government agencies in the United States. And of importance here, after reviewing sections of this book, Frank mentioned that he could see adventures in several risky career situations he'd encountered—and volunteered a brief essay on two such experiences for the Appendix (Personal Experiences of Three Adventurous Friends).

The movement through this series of responsible positions might seem strange to some—but to Frank, it was simply the result of his career/life philosophy: Change jobs every five years or so! Few of us would feel secure with such career mobility, but Frank thrived on it.

In retirement his adventurous spirit has led him into a continuous series of demanding writing projects: An extensive family history; publication of hundreds of letters he wrote to his parents during military service in Europe during World War II; and histories of both the WPAC and the FEI. Add to that his countless essays on politics and government sent by e-mail to an unbelievably long list of friends and colleagues—and you have a picture of a truly adventurous spirit living life to the fullest.

Frank and his equally adventurous wife, Suzie, move among three different residences: Florida in the winter; Vermont in the summer; and Annapolis, Maryland in the fall and spring. We always manage to meet for lunch when they are in Annapolis. At our last lunch Frank gave me a copy of his latest book on family stories. And, today he sent one of his e-mails to the world saying he and Suzie were buying a new home in Florida.

Always working, seeking new experiences, and at the age of 92 still playing tennis and raving to me about the great walking paths near his new home. Need I say more about this truly adventurous spirit?

Colonel Robert J. Gerard, Ph.D.

I first met Bob in 1963, when we were army officers and neighbors attending the US Army Command and General Staff College at Fort Leavenworth, Kansas. I encountered him again in the late 1970s when we served on the faculty of the US Army War College in Carlisle, Pennsylvania. In 1980 I retired from the Army and began a second career as Chair, Department of Business and Economics at Mount Saint Mary's College (now University) in Emmitsburg, Maryland. A few years later, needing to hire a professor of management, I contacted Bob and persuaded him to join me on our faculty.

Bob was great—in everything he ever did. As an infantry officer and pilot with three years in combat (one in Korea and two in Vietnam) he'd had more than enough adventures to satisfy most mortals. But his move to Mount Saint Mary's College sparked a whole new set of interests. He became, in short order, one of the most outstanding faculty members on campus—beloved by his students and highly respected by fellow faculty throughout the college. But I write about him here, because of a goal he set for himself just before retiring from teaching. Bob had two masters degrees, but did not have a doctorate. So, at an age when many people retire, and with nothing to gain professionally, he entered the doctoral program in public administration at Penn State University and received his Ph.D. after retiring from Mount Saint Mary's College (now University).

Think for a moment about this undertaking in the context of this book's definition of adventure, and I think you will agree: This was indeed a most demanding intellectual adventure, deserving a place in our collection here.

Father Henry B. Haske, S.J.

Father Haske was a Jesuit priest and a boyhood and life-long friend. He recently died, I'm sad to say; but he richly deserves a place in this book. Ordained in 1957 at age thirty, he did, by any measure, lead a life of adventure—starting with his first assignment: Establishing, with five others, an elementary and high school in Chile and serving there for eleven years—and then holding progressively more responsible positions within the Jesuit Order, for over four decades.

But two of his adventures in recent years will be my focus here. About four years ago, at age 80, Father Haske mentioned to me that he was considering retiring from active ministry. And he did briefly sample retired life; but, as I had expected, he found it not to his liking. So he accepted an offer to join the staff of Scranton Prep, a Jesuit high school in Pennsylvania. His charter was to create his own set of responsibilities. And did he ever!

I visited him several times at Scranton Prep and was impressed by the ease with which he had become a valued member of the community. He made himself very available to students, said a daily Mass that drew both students and faculty, was an ardent attendee at all social and athletic events—and, when you walked the halls with him, you sensed mutual respect and affection, as he exchanged greetings with everyone.

For most "ex-retirees" this life would seem adventure enough—but not for Father Haske. He added a truly innovative task to his responsibilities. As mentioned earlier in the section on Paul Mariani's spiritual adventure, at the center of Jesuit spirituality is a thirty day silent retreat designed hundreds of years ago by Saint Ignatius Loyola, founder of the Order. Over his long career, Father Haske had directed countless thirty day Ignation retreats for both Jesuit priests and lay people, guiding them through the spiritual Exercises.

At Scranton Prep, he experimented with alternative approaches for lay people to experience the Exercises—formats that do not require individuals to disengage from their normal lives for thirty days to experience the spiritual benefits of the Exercises. What started as an experiment with a few interested lay faculty at the school grew to include interested parents and students. During the 2012 Lenten period, twenty-five parents and thirty-two senior class students participated, guided through the Exercises by eleven retreat directors trained by Father Haske. Quite an achievement, quite an adventure.

But there is still more to tell about my remarkable friend. In the summer of 2011 he volunteered to spend two months in Wyoming, providing religious services to staff and visitors at three locations in Yellowstone National Park. Austere accommodations, long rough drives over unimproved roads, and occasional encounters with wild animals—all were part of this priest's "summer adventure."

And now my friend is on the greatest adventure of all—God Bless!

Colonel Peter B. Petersen, DBA and Colonel Paul W. Child, Jr.

These two friends from army days and beyond have unusual adventure stories to tell. Pete's took place in China during one quite stressful 24 hour period; and Paul's involves dozens of travel expeditions, to include an effort to involve his many children and grandchildren in adventure trips with him. Their stories take some time and space to tell, so I accepted their offers to prepare essays which you can find in the Appendix (Personal Stories of Three Adventurous Friends—which also includes an essay by my friend, Frank Sherwood, as I mentioned earlier). They are fascinating stories that I know you will enjoy.

To this short chapter devoted to five friends, I would be remiss if I did not acknowledge that there are dozens of other friends I could have included. They include people with involvement in any and all of the types of adventures recounted in the book. But they also, too often, include something more—the adventure of picking up one's life and carrying on after a harsh life setback or tragedy. I have seen so many friends and relatives exhibit such courage in the face of illness and loss of loved ones. An adventure can sometimes be seen as simply doing one's best in impossible situations. I have seen my share of it through the stories of many friends.

Part II

Conclusions:
Mining the Evidence

Chapter 6

Conclusions

You've been reading about a wide range of adventure activities and remarkable adventurers. In this chapter I won't repeat all the earlier discussion—but simply highlight some of the dominant motivations of the various groups and individuals. So, let's look at them one-by-one.

Six Groups of Adventurers

- Astronauts
  - o Push technological boundaries
  - o Practice their craft
  - o Excitement and joy
  - o Chart new worlds

- Mountain Climbers
  - o Push physical limits
  - o Encounter mystical experiences
  - o Danger and excitement
  - o Sensual appreciation of the mountains
  - o Experience a metaphor for all of life

- Runners
  - o Test endurance and tolerance for pain
  - o Gain self-knowledge
  - o Comradeship
  - o Fitness

- Writers
  - o Learn something new
  - o Share knowledge or a story
  - o Experience a unique lifestyle

- Readers
    - Escape and joy
    - Gain insights into life and the wider world
    - Learn new things

- Travelers
    - Experience new places and new people
    - Experience danger, fun, joy
    - Gain a feeling of accomplishment

Six Famous Adventurers

- Sir Ernest Shackleton
    - Urge to discover
    - Thrill of going
    - Satisfaction of learning
    - Test his capacity to endure hardship

- Amelia Earhart
    - Practice her craft
    - Push boundaries—of flight, of women
    - Fun

- Jackie Robinson
    - Pursue excellence in baseball
    - Eliminate racial barriers

- Martin Luther King, Jr.
    - Advance his dream of racial equality
    - Support the Civil Rights Movement

- Pope John XXIII
    - Modernize the Catholic Church

- Teddy Roosevelt
    - Purge his demons
    - Satisfy intense curiosity
    - Experience danger and excitement

Five Unusual Adventures

- Intellectual Adventure: A Return to the Great Books
    - o   Revisit/reexamine old ideas anew
    - o   Assess the current relevance of the Great Books
    - o   Replace restlessness with excitement

- Planning Adventure: Climbing the Seven Summits
    - o   Pursue excellence and the impossible dream
    - o   Comradeship
    - o   Test physical limits
    - o   Excitement

- Travel Adventure: Circling the Globe by Motorcycle
    - o   Satisfy a dream—to see the world
    - o   Investigate investment opportunities
    - o   Experience danger and excitement

- Sea Adventure: A Late-life Racing Crew
    - o   Test physical limits
    - o   Defy aging stereotypes
    - o   Excitement and danger
    - o   Comradeship

- Spiritual Adventure: A Thirty Day Retreat
    - o   Confront the past
    - o   Plan the future
    - o   Deepen spirituality

Five Adventurous Friends

- Frank P. Sherwood, Ph.D.
    - o   Build institutions
    - o   Share knowledge
    - o   Advance management and leadership theory

- Fr. Henry B. Haske, S.J.
    - o   Serve his Jesuit order and its institutions
    - o   Help others to enhance spirituality
    - o   Experience new environments

- Colonel Robert J. Gerard, Ph.D.
  - o Experience a demanding intellectual challenge
  - o Learning and professional development

- Colonel Paul W. Child, Jr.
  - o See the world
  - o Deepen spirituality
  - o Enrich family thru shared experiences

- Colonel Peter B. Petersen, DBA
  - o Expand intellectual and physical horizons
  - o Experience excitement and danger
  - o See the world

Ok, lists-upon-lists. Hard to get our arms around it all. So, let me try one more list—a synthesis of all that went before, into fifteen dominant motivations:

Synthesis

- Pursue excellence—through stretch goals
- Fulfill dreams
- Experience excitement, fun, joy, danger, and comradeship
- Push personal and technological boundaries
- Learn
- Share knowledge
- Seek a wider world
- Satisfy curiosity
- Deal with adversity and setbacks
- Experience unique lifestyles
- Escape the status quo
- Right wrongs; further causes
- Reform or serve institutions
- Exercise leadership
- Develop spiritually

As I reflect on these conclusions—this list of 15 motivations—I am struck by the diversity of reasons for the pursuit of adventure. When I look inward I realize that many of these motivations do not apply to me. But some do.

And I suspect that some apply to you, and this is important—to you, and to the intent of this book. Recall my definition of adventure: the pursuit of a goal beyond one's reach. And my objective with this book: to encourage others to seek adventure as a way to enrich their lives.

So in conclusion, let me suggest that we all take time to reflect on the adventures contained in this book and the motivations that drove them—as a lens to examine our own life goals and motivations, and the possibilities to achieve them through adventures of our choice.

Part III

Personal Adventures

Chapter 7

Reflections on Past Adventures

My life has had many parts, twists, and turns. I spent 29 years as an army officer, 22 as a college professor, and 20 as a management consultant during my teaching career. Now in retirement I write books. On reflection, it now seems like one long adventure—so worth noting in this book.

In the army I had a wide variety of command and staff assignments both in the United States and overseas. During my service, my family moved 20 times—adventure enough for most people.

Knowing I would have to retire after 30 years of service, I spent the last four years of service studying part-time for a doctorate in preparation for a second career in college teaching and consulting in the areas of management and leadership. Finally, in the past ten years I've written four books in that teaching area.

I have truly loved my life and the variety of experiences it has brought me. I was helped so much along the way by many wonderful friends, colleagues, and bosses; by a wife who was always ready for the next adventure; by three children and eight grandchildren I admire, respect, and love; and by a lot of just plain good luck.

But there were some very dark spots as well. I lost my wife, Pat, to cancer in 1999 and a 14 year old granddaughter, Caroline, to the same disease in 2008. And I had a personal bout with cancer in 2003.

Those were sad times, saddest in my life—made bearable by only one thing: The memory of the extraordinary courage and nobility of Pat and Caroline, whom I adore, and the love and devotion of my family and some very special friends who gave their all to help me, Pat, Caroline, and one another.

Why do I recount all this? Simple purpose. Writing this book has made me see so much of my life as an adventure. The junctures in my long career had many decision points—times when I chose to try something unknown; choices that often involved risks. I would not have wanted to miss these exciting experiences.

As for the tragic experiences of losing two loved ones, these too were adventures—of the spirit. I would have given anything to have spared Pat, Caroline, and my family from all that happened. But I must also acknowledge that, through these experiences, I have witnessed a degree of courage and love that has changed my own view of life for the better. To see such nobility in the people I so love, has brought some measure of consolation—an appreciation for having such remarkable people in my life—to simply have known them. Small consolation, but it is all I have, so I treasure it.

Chapter 8

Future Adventures

I must confess. This project has done for me exactly what I hoped it might do for you: inspired a new adventure.

As soon as I put this book to rest I'm going to tackle this new venture—an intellectual adventure that I've been thinking about for over thirty years: My Book Year.

When I was working on my doctorate in the late 1970s, I often ate lunch with a very imaginative group of fellow students. We were buried in work, specifically in the over 100 books required in our program. But often we talked about wanting to eventually have the time, money, and freedom to have a Book Year: a year in which we would read widely in areas of our choosing, for the pure love of books.

Well, I now have that opportunity, and I'm going to do it. Even now, while finishing this book, I'm tinkering with the idea—making lists of interest areas and specific books. Once this book is in print, I'll pursue this task in earnest for a year, and then write about the experience—as still another adventure!

Epilogue

Epilogue

As you and I finish this book, I'd like to ask you to reflect once again on my earlier definition of adventure. It is the pursuit of any goal that may be beyond our reach. The nature of the adventure—physical, emotional, intellectual, or even spiritual—is unimportant. But adventure always involves stepping out of our comfort zone and pushing our limits. And it always carries the risk of failure. In one sense, the uncertainty is what characterizes every adventure and drives every adventurer.

I've told you the stories of many others to illustrate the extraordinary range of possible adventure activities and motivations. Why?—To help you extend your thinking of possible adventures—for you.

I've also shared with you some of my own life story—adventures past and future. Why?—To inspire you to never give up in the search for new adventures, the key to a richer life.

And one last thought. What's to stop us? I think it might be the false perception that age is the ultimate barrier. Should that be of concern to you, take encouragement from these famous lines by Alfred Lord Tennyson in his poem *Ulysses*:

> *Come, my friends. Tis not too late to seek a newer world . . .*
>
> *Tho' much is taken, much abides; and tho' we are not now that strength which in old days moved earth and heaven; that which we are, we are; one equal temper of heroic hearts, made weak by time and fate, but strong in will to strive, to seek, to find, and not to yield.*

So . . . Drive on!

Appendix

Personal Stories
of Three Adventurous Friends

Some Adventures Have Risks So Act Accordingly

(Story of one eventful day in Red China)

By Colonel Peter B. Petersen, DBA

The Call of Strange Places

(Story of a lifetime of travel)

By Colonel Paul W. Child, Jr.

Career Risks as Adventures

By Dr. Frank P. Sherwood, Ph.D.

Some Adventures Have Risks
So Act Accordingly

By Peter B. Petersen

If you prefer adventure to the familiarity and comforts of home, this story may be of interest. In my 80 years, I have had quite a few adventures which I would like to share with readers such as making 80 parachute jumps; visiting Tibet; traveling to Antarctica; seeing Cuba while Castro ruled; and, at age 65, reaching the summit of Mount Kilimanjaro. My story here involves China during the upheaval of 1989.

Although I love adventure, I do acknowledge that some adventures can have risks such as personal injury and possible imprisonment. For example, illegally crossing the border into Iran during the past three decades would not have been wise. Consequently, the smart traveler should be aware of the current status of political and public safety conditions and act responsibly. The adventure presented here provides a few lessons learned that may be helpful. Most importantly, these actions did not violate the laws of the host country and I acted responsibly.

The adventure described in this story takes place during the beginning of June 1989 when a series of events led to the brutal massacre in Tiananmen Square in the Peoples Republic of China. I had been scheduled to present a paper in Hong Kong and in Beijing during June 11-21, 1989 when the Eastern Academy of Management and the People's University of China planned a joint session. Scholars presented their papers in Hong Kong while government officials cancelled the portion scheduled in Beijing involving the People's University of China due to the widespread uprising and subsequent massacre.

After learning that the Eastern Academy of Management's presentations in Beijing were cancelled, my wife and I boarded a taxi to the Hong Kong airport to inquire about flight options for traveling in Asia outside of The Peoples Republic of China; indeed, the sudden alteration in my scholarly travel meant we were now on vacation. With our unexpected change in plans, we hoped to be able to voyage to Malaysia or Singapore for the first time. Along with these questions, I wanted to inquire about the possibility of going to nearby Guangzhou (historically known as Canton), about 180 miles inland from Hong Kong. This area interested me as it was a significant treaty port open to foreign trade after the Opium War of 1839-1842. In fact, during the mid-1800s Canton was a major center of commerce where foreign ships would arrive at Hong Kong then travel inland on the Pearl River and conduct their business in Canton. I imagined these 19th century ships and visualized myself dining at the famous White Swan Hotel on the banks of the Pearl River in Guangzhou. My wife, however, was dead-set against me traveling in China under the current political conditions.

At the airport, the authorities appeared friendly and eager to assist foreign travelers. In the normal course of events, I struck up a conversation with a Chinese pilot, fluent in English, who had just arrived on a Chinese Airline and appeared to be completing routine paperwork. Realizing that the government of The Peoples Republic of China was attempting to project the notion that everything had returned to normal, I stated, "I guess that aircraft are no longer departing Hong Kong for China?" He responded, "We are open for business and you can board a flight now if you wish. And the trains are also running."

After we returned to our hotel we enjoyed a rather quiet evening that included a delicious meal in a local restaurant. However, the excitement began the next morning when I dressed in a hurry and started out the door. My dear wife, who I have been married to now for 58 years, shouted out, "You are not going into China. I'll be darned if I'll wait here for seven years for Red China to release you." As I moved into the hall quickly she attempted to stop me but I had the advantage of being fully dressed while she was still in her nightgown. I ran downstairs and was out on the street a moment later. Arriving by cab at the train station the driver commented that it looked deserted and that trains were probably all cancelled; further, he suggested that I ride back to my hotel with him. Disregarding the driver's advice, I entered the train station and headed to the ticket counter. Wooden barriers to hold back crowds and keep people in line were in place but not needed because at the moment I was the only potential passenger.

As I approached the ticket counter the three or four attendants present suddenly seemed to be very busy and unable to wait on me. In a moment or two, I addressed one of them and requested, "May I purchase a round trip ticket to Guangzhou?" He responded, "Sorry, no speak English." After similar responses, one of them, when asked directly, finally said, "one way only." In 1989, during a significant disturbance in China can you imagine buying a one way ticket into The People's Republic of China? I answered, "Yes, but where do I purchase a ticket for the return trip?" He answered matter of factly, "At the train station in Guangzhou." Then after buying the ticket to Guangzhou I learned from English speaking Chinese passengers who were now arriving that I would need Chinese currency in Guangzhou. In fact, my US colleagues at the conference advised wrongly that the Chinese government preferred US dollars. Although individual entrepreneurs might prefer dollars, government institutions such as the railroads only accept official currency. Consequently, before I could purchase a return ticket I needed to acquire Chinese money. Complicating matters passengers started moving towards the train preparing to depart for Guangzhou. Since it seemed that I could not solve these matters at Kowloon, why not take a seat, relax, and enjoy the trip?

A seat assignment had been printed on my ticket so I headed in that direction and took a seat. Other travelers trying to be helpful gestured that I move to an alternative seat. Then in a few moments the conductor had me move to a third location. Looking out the window several neatly dressed women in Army uniforms, looking quite official and seemingly impressed with their own importance, walked up and down the platform and looked the equivalent of an American corporal with a clipboard.[1] I remained in my seat and the train soon departed from British Kowloon. As the train entered The Peoples Republic of China, it became obvious to me that the Chinese took their security very seriously; indeed, the size and apparent weight of the huge doors to the railroad entrance and exit appeared daunting. As part of these fortifications, large spikes covered the wall and the doors.

After crossing the frontier the train picked up speed, people settled back in their chairs, and soon it was tea time. Two older passengers came to my rescue using only pantomime to communicate that I should hold out my issued Styrofoam cup containing dry tea leaves while one of them poured boiling water into the cup. After the tea steeped and cooled it was a refreshing drink. Then the ladies insisted that I should save both the cup and what was left of the soggy tea leaves for a second and third round of the beverage. It dawned on me then that their earlier gestures about changing seats were attempted in order to find a better seat for me to observe their countryside. In the end, the conductor, who also wanted to help, found an even better seat for this foreigner.

---

[1]   After spending an earlier but lengthy career in the US Army, I realized that you "don't mess" with a corporal with a clipboard and acted accordingly.

We passed farms, residential dwellings, and light industry sites. As we approached Guangzhou, my destination, it looked similar to downtown Seoul, Korea during the 1970s. Most of the structures and all of the elevated roadways that I saw were made out of concrete giving a solid drab grayish look to this portion of the city. Exiting the train and station, I decided that it would be wise to do whatever required a taxi first and then get back to the station by late afternoon in time for a train back to Kowloon. As I stepped into the crowd in front of the station, cab drivers shouted in their native tongue recruiting fares. Not knowing how to speak Chinese, I felt out of place and was relieved when a cab driver spoke to me in German. Fortunately, he also spoke English and mentioned that many Americans had departed the city because of the situation.

Since it was noontime, I asked the driver to join me for lunch at the White Swan Hotel and then drive me back to the train station. He did not want to leave his vehicle unattended but agreed to park and wait outside for me; however, I first had to tip the doorman to permit the cab to loiter near the hotel. With that hurdle accomplished, I entered the hotel and headed towards the restaurant. Although I found it to be almost empty, a lady in her early 50's paid her bill and made a hasty retreat upon my entrance. She appeared to be the wife of an Eastern European bureaucrat who did not feel like associating with a Westerner. Nonetheless, I enjoyed good service and a great meal. Once fortified with food I was ready to deal with trying to legally convert my currency and buy a ticket back to Kowloon.

Arriving back at the train station I quickly found both the ticket counters as well as the banks closed. At a loss for what to do, I recalled that if you have difficulties in an autocratic environment, your best bet is to go to the police station and complain about it. Subsequently, your problems will be solved or perhaps they will throw you in jail. Since the national government was announcing to the foreign press that everything in China had returned to normal, a complaint at the police station seemed like an ideal solution. The walk to the station allowed me some time to contemplate what I was going to request.

The local police station was neat and orderly and run by a smiling woman with the rank of sergeant. After hearing my tale of woe, she took me to the bank and woke up some of the staff who exchanged my money. Then we walked to the train station, and woke up some of the staff who sold me a ticket to Kowloon. Problems solved, I thanked her and headed to the outside waiting area. Later I learned that the employees had been on a mid-day siesta and both businesses would have been opened if I had bided my time and waited about another hour. With ticket in hand, I rested in a shady spot on the outside train platform and was the target of a minor sting operation. In fact it came in three distinct phases and would become one of the most exciting parts of my day.

Initially, I found myself in the position of being tempted to break the law or be disrespectful to the Peoples Republic of China through encouragement to criticize the government and verbally support the rebellious protesters. To this end I was approached by a well-dressed older gentleman looking like a Hollywood version of a modern Chinese professor. Wearing a sport jacket, neatly pressed trousers and a shirt with a collar but no necktie, he asked about my awareness of rioting in Beijing and offered that he would be most interested in my reaction. The gist of my response was that I was a busy tourist who was not up-to-date on the latest current events; consequently, I had no reaction. Eventually, he walked away without catching a foreign devil.

After a while I was approached by a sleazy young man who resembled what was often referred to as a slicky boy during the 1950s and 1960s; that is, low level black marketers, sellers of drugs, and minor criminals. However, in Asia and the United States these young men are now a very small fraction of the population. This man in particular played his part well, initially offering to provide me with some recent photos of Chinese motor vehicles parked in a local military motor pool. Rather than give way to temptation and ask for photos of the latest night vision devices used by the Chinese infantry, I rejected whatever he might have to offer and asked for nothing. As he faded away I realized how hot and humid it was getting. It seemed that the abundant concrete was soaking up the heat.

For a moment, I reflected on the significance of today's date; June 14, 1989. It was my middle son's birthday, the US Army's birthday, and also Flag Day in honor of Old Glory. For The Peoples Republic of China, today marked the 10th day after the high point of activity related to the Tiananmen Square massacre in Beijing. The government had tolerated the minor misbehavior of students who had challenged their nation's leaders but responded with brutal force when major portions of the population supported them.

As the afternoon wore on I had a third visitor in the three act sting operation. A fairly attractive woman in her mid-20's approached me wearing tight jeans, a short sleeve polo shirt, and sneakers. The memorable part of her outfit was the word SPORTS (whatever that meant) embroidered on her polo shirt. Her game was to offer to visit with unaccompanied male tourists in a quiet and secluded place nearby and pass the time until the train arrived. My response was a clear and firm, "NO Thanks". A moment later I noticed the professor, slicky boy, and Ms. Sports conferring and comparing notes. The professor, to no surprise, was leading the three-person meeting.

Apparently I passed the course because they disappeared shortly thereafter. In fact, the train station itself seemed rather empty and I wondered if my train had been canceled. Later I learned that passengers who arrived hours early like I did avoided hanging out at the train station. Instead during those days of heightened security during the Tiananmen Square incident they lingered somewhere near the station and then dashed to the station just as the train arrived. Indeed, this approach was used by many to lessen their chances of being questioned by the authorities. However, one attractive Caucasian woman in her mid 20's wearing jeans, a pull-over short sleeve blouse, and sneakers did arrive early pushing a small baggage wagon that she later used to move large pouches to her vehicle. Neatly groomed with one long pigtail, I would have bet that she was from a consulate of a Western nation coming to pick up pouches of mail from the train.

Late in the afternoon, my train arrived on schedule and hundreds of people wanting to purchase a ticket and board the train arrived from the neighborhood simultaneously. About half of them were Chinese civilians and the rest Westerners, mostly in their 20's, many accompanied by their young families. Husbands usually carried a foot locker or large suitcase and had their eldest child by the hand. Often wives followed carrying one or two young children as well as a suitcase and purse. The overwhelming sentiment of the Westerners seemed to be, "get me out of this place." I asked one African man who was straining under the load of a heavy foot locker, "Where are you from?" While continuing to run by he responded, "The London School." I would later learn that he was in China as part of a doctoral program at the London School of Economics.

As the train came to a halt and the doors were about to be opened, a platoon or two of Chinese soldiers arrived and positioned themselves in a linear formation between the train and the passengers waiting to board. They wore mixed uniforms; that is generally military shirts, civilian pants, and well-worn sneakers. Local militia such as this is often a rag-tag outfit with few skills, little discipline, and no comparison with the highly professional regular army component of the People's Liberation Army.[2]

Once the train doors opened the male students inside the train shouted defiantly at the soldiers and the female students by and large screamed at the top of their voices. They boldly wore temporary tattoos of their negative opinions of the government on their faces and arms written with indelible ink pens the equivalent of Magic Markers. The unarmed militia punched and pushed many of the students in the face and upper body as they exited the train. I do not recall if they carried a stick or even a policemen's night stick; however, the emphasis was in trying to punch and push students. It seemed no doubt to me that these students were being beat-up by mean spirited thugs. As the beatings ensued, two teams of noise makers joined the militia, carrying empty plastic soda bottles sealed with their used caps. When stomped on the ground they made a sound similar to a fire cracker, adding to the confusion. However, this noise and brutality did not frighten the courageous students.

The militia's fury at the students had been incensed days earlier by students who killed soldiers in Beijing and hung their bodies from a bridge. Clearly, these two groups despised each other. For the soldiers, there was no discrimination in their beatings because of gender. A young woman at arm's length from me was punched in the face, fell to the ground, was then helped up, punched again, fell down and was kicked while lying on the ground. I noticed previously that she had been particularly expressive in her shouting at the soldiers.

The beatings lasted from 20 to 30 minutes or as long as it took for the last man and woman to leave the train. Realizing that they were outmatched, students usually limited their opposition to shouting insults at the soldiers. Subsequently the militia apprehended several of the more engaged students and escorted them from the station. For the other students, June 14th was ten days after the high point of activity and now they were evacuating their colleges and the capital and returning to their homes throughout the nation. While the Beijing authorities welcomed their departure, the students' parents and other members of their extended families were probably relieved to have them safe at home.

---

[2]   In fairness to the poorly dressed militia, their attire was suitable for the ensuing street brawl while more formal uniforms would be useful on the parade ground.

Now in their early 40s, many of these former students probably remember their return home from Beijing on June 14, 1989 and the beating they received from the local militia. Some who received broken noses and broken teeth are reminded today when they look in the mirror. Many other people throughout the world recall two photographs connected with this event in Tiananmen Square. In one photo a Chinese student stood in front of a column of tanks and refused to let them proceed. The other photo is of an impromptu built statue representing their demands; liberty. To Westerners the statue looked like a combination of the Statue of Liberty and Quan Yin, the Asian goddess of mercy. About 30 feet tall and made out of lightweight material, the statue became part of their demonstrations and its white covering represented the many young people who participated in the event some giving their lives. Unlike the Statue of Liberty, the Chinese figure held her torch aloft with both hands.

Once my train loaded, it embarked with passengers both seated and standing.[3] When the train passed through the short frontier tunnel from China to British Kowloon, it seemed that everyone on the train gave a sigh of relief. I will not forget the brutal and mindless way the local militia in Guangzhou acted toward the students returning home from Tiananmen Square. These soldiers seemed out of control as they beat these defenseless young people. After disembarking, I returned to our hotel and apologized to my dear wife. Fortunately she forgave me and after I got cleaned up we went out to eat and I relayed the day's events. Other students newly arrived from Beijing crowded the Hong Kong restaurant and everyone seemed to have a story to tell. Indeed, it had been a busy day filled with excitement and adventure.

---

[3] Just before we boarded the train for our return trip to Kowloon, I was surprised to find neatly dressed technicians operating metal detectors to screen all passengers. Further, that these machines appeared to be similar to the state of the art devices then in operation in 1989 at US airports.

The Call of Strange Places

By Paul W. Child, Jr.

My friend of many decades, John Hook, knowing a good deal about my life and adventures, asked me to provide a short essay for his book, and I am more than happy to oblige. Not only am I happy to help John, but I have found preparing the work a satisfying journey through memory lane—something of an adventure in itself.

> Faraway places with strange sounding names
> Faraway over the sea
> Those faraway places with strange sounding names
> Are calling, calling me

> Faraway Places
> By Alex Kramer and Joan Whitney

Let me begin my account by stating that my story is distinctly not about an individual of special talents, but rather about one who has been drawn to faraway places and has found himself blessed with a steady stream of unique adventures since boyhood. Perhaps it all began with inheriting the genes of my grandparents. At one point in her life my grandmother Child packed up my Aunt Helen and my father when they were small tykes and in a horse-drawn wagon headed from Sioux Falls to western South Dakota to lay a claim on some frontier land, where they lived in a sod hut for a year. My grandparents Bicek found their way from Czechoslovakia to New Prague, Minnesota, where they established a small farm. So in a real sense I inherited a love of travel, new adventures, and the seeking out of exotic places.

Like most of us, my life has moved through a series of phases. Real adventures began for me when my father dropped me off at a meeting of Boy Scout Troop 39 on my 12th birthday. The scoutmaster, Tony Sikorski, and his assistant, Pop Gregory, had a good deal to do with my life for the next 8 years, Then followed the special opportunities provided as a cadet at the United States Military Academy (USMA), a career as an army officer, a staff member of the USMA Association of Graduates, and finally, after full retirement, an adventure travel program of my own. And during these latter days, on most of these excursions I was accompanied by family members—my good wife Judy, one of our six children, and more recently one of our many grandchildren.

Scouting introduced me to the outdoor world, which began with a cold, autumn weekend campout at Newton Hills, a rough backwoods area near Canton, South Dakota. Then followed over the years summers on the camp staff at Lake Shetek in southwestern Minnesota; but scouting also took me into the Boundary Waters of Canada on an extended canoe trip, and west on a trek through the Black Hills of South Dakota. Later as a West Point cadet I experienced a number of engaging excursions during the summer, often to other military posts. And when at Fort Bliss we had the opportunity to visit Juarez, Mexico. And as one would expect, a career in the army provided many fascinating visits to foreign lands including Japan, Korea and Europe (Germany, France, England, Greece, and Crete).

After retiring from the army I had the very good fortune of joining the staff of West Point's Association of Graduates (AOG). After arriving at their offices at the Academy, I learned that the AOG had an excellent travel program for graduates and their wives. Members of the staff and their wives were assigned to the various trips to see that things went smoothly. Our director, Bob Lamb, did a fine job of making the arrangements. Judy's and my initial voyage was a paddlewheel boat excursion up the Mississippi River from New Orleans to St. Louis, with interesting stops along the way. As an additional feature, we found ourselves in a race with a group of Naval Academy graduates in a similar boat. Happily, we won by a hair. In the seven years that followed we found ourselves with congenial groups touring Alaska, the Panama Canal, Egypt, and a final trip through all of Scandinavia.

In the mid-1980's I was able to begin a series of adventure trips, usually sponsored by a competent travel agency. The Far East has for some reason always held a special attraction for me, especially the Himalayas. I did enjoy completing seven treks in various sections of Nepal, and either before or after a trek there would be stop-offs in India, Thailand, China, Tibet, Hong Kong, or Burma (Myanmar). Closer to home were a number of canoe voyages with Outward Bound or Wilderness Inquiry. And more recently, a trek in Peru from Cusco to Machu Picchu on the Inca Trail with my good friend Steven LeBlanc, a highly experienced traveler who operates an adventure travel agency. Then with another traveling companion, Tom Warth, the founder of Books for Africa, I went first to Tanzania and the Kilimanjaro area in Africa, and later on the Trans-Siberian train trip from

Moscow to Beijing. Last summer found us on a trek through Utah's Arches and Canyon's territory.

I have also been blessed with a spiritual dimension to my life. That actually began as a scout at Camp Shetek, where our chaplain, Father Berrum, became a close friend over the years. Sadly, he passed away early from polio a year before the vaccine was developed. Another priest, Father McPhillips, also a scouter, became a friend, and actually drove me from South Dakota to enter the Academy in the summer of 1948. At West Point, Fathers Moore and McCormick introduced me to the writings of Thomas Merton, a monk at Gethsemani Monastery in Kentucky. I was delighted to learn much later that one could make extended, silent retreats there. So a few years back, I began making annual retreats there, sometimes spending as much as a month with the monks. They were especially kind to me, especially Brother Rene, inviting me to participate in all of their activities. I would be given a place in the choir, and worked with them in their fudge shop. No question about it, those tranquil days at Gethsemani enriched my spiritual life. There were also weekend retreats at various other places, and when in the Orient, I usually stopped by the Buddhist monasteries, where listening to the chants of their monks also added to my spiritual experience.

John suggested that in my contribution I should consider providing a list, without extended comment, of some of the places I have been and perhaps noting any special interests involved. So here goes:

Africa: Tanzania, Zanzibar, Kilimanjaro (Hemingway's The Snows of Kilimanjaro)

Alaska: Anchorage, Fairbanks, Juneau, Mount McKinley

Burma (Myanmar): Rangoon, Mandalay (and other Kipling sites)

Canada: Boundary Waters, Blood Vein River, Winnipeg, Toronto

China: Peking, Shanghai, Hong Kong, Chingdu, Nanning (the triplets that our daughter Mary Julia and her husband David adopted came from an orphanage in Nanning)

Egypt: Alexandria, Cairo, Aswan Dam, the Pyramids, the Sphinx, cruise on the Nile

England: London, Shakespeare sites, other historical sites

France: Paris (Shakespeare & Company Bookstore), Notre Dame Cathedral, Eiffel Tower, Gertrude Stein sites (the Lost Generation spokesperson)

Greece: Athens (the Acropolis and other historical sites), Corinth and other places of religious interest, Crete (burial site of Nikos Kazantzakis)

India: Dehli (Gandhi sites), Agra (Taj Mahal), many historical forts, religious sites

Ireland: Dublin, Sligo (Yeats sites), Galway, Aran Islands (John Synge sites), Belfast

Italy: Assisi (sites of St. Francis), Rome (St. Peter's Cathedral and other religious sites), Florence (statue of David)

Japan: Tokyo, Kobe, Kyoto, Osaka, Yokohama

Mexico: Juarez, Puerto Allen, Acapulco, Cancun, Tres Marias (kayaking on ocean)

Nepal: Kathmandu (helped out at Mother Teresa's home for the elderly), Langtang (1st trek—on the Tibetan border), Annapurna (3 treks—most beautiful), Namche Bazaar, Everest region, Pokhara, western Nepal (Snow Leopard country)

Scandinavia: Denmark, Finland, Norway, Sweden

Tibet: Lhasa (the Potala), other Dalai Lama and Buddhist sites

Trans-Siberian Train Ride: from Moscow to Peking, Russia, Mongolia, Siberia, Lake Baikal

Wales: Dylan Thomas sites (son Bill with me—he was collecting material for his master's thesis on Thomas)

There were other places, but they have now faded from my memory.

Almost all of our travels these days include the company of a grandchild. I might close this essay by mentioning three recent adventures. I had taken grandson Eddie, 16 years old, on an excursion to Ireland that was quite successful. He melded in very well with the elderly. So I decided to take him with me on a Franciscan pilgrimage to Assisi and Rome. Again he proved himself an excellent traveling companion. Among other ventures, we climbed to the top of a cathedral in Florence and to the top of St. Peter's in Rome. The stairs were narrow and steep, but his steady, strong young arm got us both to the top of each place—an exhilarating feat that we will each remember down through the years.

Eddie's younger brother Emmet was interested in seeing Holland, so I managed a very fine trip that took us to London, Paris, and then Amsterdam. He also proved to be a good traveling companion. A high point occurred on a boat ride on a canal in Amsterdam. The kind pilot turned the wheel over to Emmet for some 30 minutes; the canal was anything but straight, but he did a memorable job of steering the craft.

Granddaughter Phoebe, thanks to her other grandparents, had seen a bit of the world, particularly China and France. So she requested an outdoor adventure in the US. I was able to arrange a Wilderness Inquiry canoe trip down the Missouri River in Montana for Phoebe, her mother Polly and myself. Neither had had any experience paddling a canoe or camping out at night, but they adjusted very nicely. The trip featured stopping at places where Lewis and Clark had camped. Phoebe had prepared herself by doing considerable reading on the adventures of the explorers, and was actually able to teach our guides some things they had not known. Again, a very memorable adventure.

> *Going to China or maybe Siam*
> *I want to see for myself*
> *Those faraway places I've been reading about*
> *In a book that I took from the shelf*

Faraway Places

Well, John, there you have it. Thanks so much for asking me to participate in what I am certain will be a fine book, and for being such a treasured friend over these many years as we shared assignments together at the Academy, in Germany, and at Carlisle Barracks.

Career Risks as Adventures

By Frank P. Sherwood

Adventuring involves moving into the unknown, with all the risks that may involve. It is also highly uncertain. The literature warns leaders that they should see their world as replete with ambiguity. In other words, they should feel comfortable when they don't really know what they are doing or why.

I have had a couple of experiences that seem to fit these circumstances, neither of which occurred in exotic foreign locales but very much happened on home territory.

Federal Executive Institute

One involved the establishment of an organization in the US government, the Federal Executive Institute (FEI), by President Lyndon B. Johnson in 1968. The FEI was to do something that had never been done before: provide education and development for the 10,000 people then at the top of a Federal bureaucracy of over 3,000,000 people.

A simple enough mandate? Not quite. What made anyone think that these 10,000 people felt they needed education and improvement? While many were highly educated and experienced, most had not been in a school room for a long time. And they had shouldered substantial management responsibilities, which were far different from their earlier education. Yet they were busy people. How could they be expected to go back to school, even for a couple months?

There were other uncertainties. I had agreed to leave my position as Director of the School of Public Administration at the University of Southern California, which I had held for only a year, to head the new enterprise. Required was a move of the family from Los Angeles to Charlottesville, Virginia. How would two teenagers deal with such an uprooting? A family decision to move settled things for the moment, but what could we expect in the long run?

How was the Institute to operate? Staff at the US Civil Service Commission, the organizational home of the new enterprise, had worked for more than a year and had produced a "Plan" for the Institute. When I read it, I flatly rejected it. If I had to follow it, I would not proceed with the job. The reason was that the Plan assumed all 10,000 executives had the same learning needs. I did not at all believe that was the case. But it was a risk to reject a plan long in the making.

It was painful and difficult to come up with an alternative that recognized individual needs would be different. The resulting curriculum was poles apart from other executive development programs. It placed great emphasis on the individual diagnosis of personal needs and provided several alternative course paths executives might pursue in meeting their personal goals. Though radically atypical, the approach met the approval of the vast majority of executives.

There was a big problem of money. The Institute was not established by the Congress but by the President. It therefore received no appropriated funds, and the President had no money to give. The Institute had to depend on fees from the agencies it served. At the beginning it lived on borrowed money, taken from some special funds, all of which had to be repaid. The market was a tough one. In the first year the Chairman of the Civil Service Commission had to function as a salesman, along with the rest of us, in order to convince reluctant agencies to provide money. Somehow we finished in the black at the end of the first year by about $7,000. It was a tough but exciting year.

The Washington Public Affairs Center of the University of Southern California

After five years at the Federal Executive Institute, I decided I wanted to return to the University, but in Washington and not in Los Angeles. I had made a big investment in the federal executives and wanted to continue working with them. My colleagues in Los Angeles and I decided we would do something that was then very unique. We would establish an outpost of the School of Public Administration in Washington, DC. For a variety of reasons, it was not as outlandish as it might sound. The School already had an outpost in Sacramento.

It was, however, a distinctive undertaking. A University located on the Pacific's shores was the first to establish a formal center and offer regular courses in the District of Columbia. Indeed, we were so ignorant we did not know we had to have a permit even to operate. The permit process was lengthy and demanding, and USC was the first one to be given such permission. There was a lot of doubt about the outcome of our request.

Money was a big problem. USC in 1973 was not a wealthy University as it is today. After much negotiation, and great help from those in the School, the University agreed to advance $60,000 for the Center. The exact terms were not specified. It was clear, however, it was an advance and not a loan. It came as quite a shock when the University asked that the advance be returned at the end of the first year. Where were our funds to come from? It was agreed that the Center would offer courses, largely on a part-time basis, to officials in the Federal government. Would they participate? We did not know. We were at the mercy of the market. The answer was provided us after we put a 10 inch advertisement in the *Washington Post*. We were inundated with calls and expressions of interest, and the Center was quickly in business.

But there was another complication. I had taught many night classes and pronounced them the worst form of education known to man. I insisted there would be no night classes at the Washington Center. But what was the alternative? How could you contrive a situation where people who worked all day could attend school?

It turned out there had been an experiment which had been ongoing at USC for about five years. It involved the consolidation of class time so that students could travel from greater distances to attend courses in Los Angeles. It had had considerable success. I had taught two of the classes and had come to believe it was a great delivery system. Why not apply it in Washington? It was so arranged. Classes met the same number of class hours for a semester credit but did it over two weekends of four days each. Students made different arrangements to handle the two workdays. USC professors from Los Angeles supplemented Center faculty by flying to DC and spending four days.

We called the program the Intensive Semester and essentially all classes were offered at the Center on this basis. It was a huge success. More than anything else, I believe, the Intensive Semester was responsible for the substantial approval the Washington Public Affairs Center enjoyed over its twenty-five year history.

I found that these two experiences, with their adventuring dimensions and high levels of ambiguity provided me more opportunities for creativity than at any other time in my life.

References

Alexander, Caroline. *The Endurance: Shackleton's Legendary Antarctic Expedition*. New York: Knopf, 1998.

Arana, Marie (Editor). *The Writing Life*. New York: Public Affairs, 2003.

Bass, Dick and Rick Ridgeway. *Seven Summits*. New York: Warner Books, 1986.

Blythe, Will (Editor). *Why I Write*. New York: Back Bay Books, 1998.

Brands, H. W. *TR: The Last Romantic*. New York: Basic Books, 1997.

Chaikin, Andrew with Victoria Kohl. *Voices From the Moon: Apollo Astronauts Describe Their Lunar Experiences*. New York: Penguin Group, 2009.

Coady, Roxanne J. and Joy Johannessen. *The Book That Changed My Life*. New York: Gotham Books, 2006.

Collins, Michael. *Liftoff: The Story of America's Adventure in Space*. New York: Grove Press 1988.

Denby, David. *Great Books*. New York: Simon & Schuster, 1996.

Editors of *Time*. *Great People of the 20th Century*. New York: Time Books, 1996.

Falls, Joe. *The Boston Marathon*. New York: Macmillan, 1977.

Johnson, Kirk. *To the Edge: A Man, Death Valley, and the Mystery of Endurance*. New York: Warner Books, 2001.

Lamb, Brian. *Booknotes: America's Finest Authors on Reading, Writing, and the Power of Ideas*. New York: Times Books, 1997.

Life. *The Greatest Adventures of All Time*. New York: Life Books, 2000.

Livingston, Gordon, MD. *And Never Stop Dancing*. New York: Marlow & Company, 2006.

References

Mariani, Paul. *Thirty Days: On Retreat with the Exercises of St. Ignatius.* New York: Viking Compass, 2002.

Morrell, Margot and Stephanie Capprell. *Shackleton's Way.* New York: Viking, 2001.

National Book Award Authors. *The Writing Life.* New York: Random House, 1995.

O'Connell, Nicholas. *Beyond Risk: Conversations with Climbers.* Seattle, Washington: The Mountaineers, 1993.

Pearl, Nancy. *Book Lust: Recommended Reading for Every Mood, Moment, and Reason.* Seattle, Washington: Sasquatch Books, 2003.

Roberts, David (Editor). *Points Unknown: The Greatest Adventure Writing on the Twentieth Century.* New York: W. W. Norton, 2000.

Rogers, Jim. *Investment Biker.* New York: Random House, 1994.

Schwartz, Ronald B. *For the Love of Books.* New York: Grosset/Putnam, 1999.

Time/CBS News. People of the Century. New York: Simon and Schuster, 1999.

About the Author

Dr. John Hook has had three diverse career experiences: an army officer for 29 years, academic for 22 years and management consultant throughout his teaching career. In the army, he served eight years overseas (in Europe, Alaska, and Vietnam); commanded units from 100 to 3,500 men; served in three different research and development agencies in Washington; taught at West Point; and chaired the Command, Leadership, and Management Department at the US Army War College. After retiring from the army in 1980, he chaired the Business and Economics Department at Mount St. Mary's College (now University) for 12 years, then remained a faculty member there for an additional 10 years. During that time, he also conducted hundreds of management seminars and provided other consulting services for public, private, and non-profit organizations, most for senior-level leaders. He has published four other books, all on management and leadership: *The Agile Manager's Guide to Influencing People; Developing Executive Skills: Managing Yourself, Others, and Organizations; Leading at the Top: Requirements for Senior Executive Effectiveness;* and *The Leadership Touch.* He is Professor Emeritus of Management at Mount St. Mary's University in Maryland.